Colorado Mountain College
Spring Valley Learning Center
Glenwood Springs, CO 81601

Husband Is the Past Tense of Daddy

ze

Husband Is the Past Tense of Daddy

And Other Dispatches from the Front Lines of Motherhood

Teryl Zarnow

ADDISON-WESLEY PUBLISHING COMPANY, INC.
Reading, Massachusetts   Menlo Park, California   New York
Don Mills, Ontario   Wokingham, England   Amsterdam
Bonn   Sydney   Singapore   Tokyo   Madrid   San Juan

Library of Congress Cataloging-in-Publication Data

Zarnow, Teryl.
    Husband is the past tense of daddy: and other dispatches
from the front lines of motherhood / Teryl Zarnow.
        p.   cm.
    ISBN 0-201-51801-5
    1. Motherhood—Humor. 2. Family—United States—
Humor.   I. Title.
HQ759.Z37   1990
306.874'3'0207—dc20
                                        90-30796
                                            CIP

Portions of this book have appeared previously in a different form in *The Orange County Register*.

Jacket design by Janet Halverson
Text design by Joyce C. Weston
Set in 11-point Meridien by DEKR Corporation,
Woburn, MA

ABCDEFGHIJ-DO-9543210
First printing, February 1990

For Zachary, Rachel, and Noah —
but especially for David:
past, present, and future.

Contents

Preface

SOMETIMES I think of my life as a series of one-act plays, but more often I see it as a situation comedy. It may be thin on plot and we may not resolve every crisis before the commercial, but my family does tend to career along in a way that would be absurd if it were not real.

You can taste the flavor of my family just by sampling our dinnertime conversation. I do not have to invent comical scripts about our dinners to sell our show as a pilot; I merely record the actual dialogue.

And that is what I do when I write. With words I try to capture the sights and sounds of these early years—years very much like our dinnertime conversations. They are as exhausting and frustrating as they are exhilarating and fulfilling and funny. Here is the script of my family at dinner:

SETTING: The family dining room.

CHARACTERS: Father, home after a hard day at the office.

Mother, serving everybody as quickly as possible.

Daughter, 3 years old, determined to be part of the conversation.

Son, 5 years old, his mouth full of questions and food.

Baby, 1 year old, just learning to eat table food. Periodically during the scene he will throw the contents of his high-chair tray onto the floor.

SON: Dad, would you tell us the story of Abraham?

FATHER: (*obviously pleased at his son's interest*) Why sure. (*Father takes a book from the shelf and begins to read.*) "Abraham was the founder of the Jewish people, the first of the Patriarchs. He discarded idol worship for belief in one God. The Covenant between God and Israel began with Abraham."

SON: (*obviously confused*) Yes, but Dad, would you tell us the story?

FATHER: I am telling you the story.

MOTHER: (*Spoken in a murmur*) Put some life into it.

SON: Can I have some more chicken?

DAUGHTER: How did Abraham get killed?

BABY: Aaaaah! (*Throws chicken on floor and begins to fuss for something else.*)

FATHER: Well, you see, Abraham and God began the Covenant for the Jewish people . . . They cut a deal.

DAUGHTER: But how did Lincoln get killed?

FATHER: That was Abraham Lincoln, he was somebody else.

SON: That's the story. Lincoln was shot in the theater.

FATHER: That's right. He was shot because somebody did not agree with his ideas. Lincoln wanted the black people to be free, but some people wanted them to be slaves. People disagreed.

MOTHER: (*serving baby and interjecting*) It was more than disagreeing. They fought a war.

FATHER: Yes, they fought about it, which wasn't a good thing to do.

SON: I bet I know which people were against slavery. The blacks were, right?

MOTHER: True. They didn't like the idea.

DAUGHTER: Well, what did Abraham do?

FATHER: Well, the Jewish people do not like slavery since they once were slaves in Egypt.

MOTHER: Well, that was really after Abraham lived.

SON: I thought Abraham was against slavery.

FATHER: Yes, Abraham Lincoln was.

DAUGHTER: Is that the story of our grandfather?

FATHER: No, that's a different Abraham. Here's a picture of your great-grandfather here on the wall. He lived in Russia.

SON: You already told us that story. He was the one who used to go everywhere selling gods from his wagon.

MOTHER: No, that was goods, not gods. The other Abraham is the one who realized there is one God.

DAUGHTER: My tummy still hurts. I'm still hungry. Can I have more chicken?

BABY: Da-da! (*Throws broccoli on floor.*)

FATHER: No, that was your other great-grandfather, not Abraham. Do you want to hear the story or not?

SON: May I be excused? I'm done eating.

MOTHER: Yes, go and read a book quietly. (*To husband*) How are you?

DAUGHTER: See the picture I made at school, Daddy?

(*The telephone rings. Father deals with solicitation to buy garbage bags to benefit shelter for abandoned dogs.*)

DAUGHTER: Daddy, see my picture!

FATHER: Yes, that's wonderful. I like it very much.

SON: Look, Mom. Remember Harry the Dirty Dog? Well, here he is in this book. Can you read me that story?

MOTHER: (*Offering cheese to baby*) After I finish my dinner. So, dear, how are you?

DAUGHTER: Can I have a piece of my Valentine candy?

SON: Yes, can I have one too?

MOTHER: All right, just one.

DAUGHTER: (*Hides candy under napkin.*) Pretend I can't find my candy, Mommy, and pretend I want another piece.

SON: (*Gets up to go into living room.*) Now can you read the story, Mom?

FATHER: Have you got chocolate on your hands? Don't go

anywhere until you wipe your hands. (*He begins clearing table.*)

DAUGHTER: Pretend, Mommy, pretend.

BABY: (*Cries loudly, translating roughly as:*) Juice, I want juice.

MOTHER: You can't have more candy. Where is the piece you had?

DAUGHTER: (*Triumphantly lifting napkin*) Here it is. I tricked you! (*Baby flings remainder of food on floor. Mother picks it up.*)

DAUGHTER: (*smiling*) So, Daddy, tell us. How are you today? End of of scene. Break to commercial.

❧

BY giving voice to my memories, I hope to preserve them. So I am Boswell to my family's Johnson; I am the lens of the video camera we have not bought. I try to write the soundtrack to what otherwise would be a silent movie.

I want to remember it all. Yet try as I might, their childhoods slip away like water through my fists. I drink in the faces of my babies as they serenely sleep, surrounded by oceans of sheet. One year later, when they dominate the crib, I am thirsty for details of how they once looked. My husband and I ask: Did she crawl like that? Was his laugh the same? Already I have forgotten exactly the first times I saw each of my children smile.

The family I began to write about three years ago has changed. My oldest son, Zachary, is now 6. He has broken the barrier of the preschool years. He is graduating kindergarten, and I have survived his first traumatic year in school. I have learned to stifle audible gasps of horror as he climbs slender trees, and he has learned (finally) to ride his bicycle without training wheels.

My daughter Rachel is now 4, but as she steers her single-minded course through life she gives every appearance of being a willful 12. Outnumbered by the men in our family, she and I are drawn close in the sisterhood of mothers and daughters. She is someone I can take shopping.

My youngest son, Noah, is now 2. He was conceived after the idea for this book. Of necessity, his is a non-speaking role. I still think of him as my baby, but he runs more than he walks in his scramble to keep up with the big kids. He is still sweet—especially since now, mercifully, he sleeps through the night.

My husband and I, intact this year of our 15th wedding anniversary, also scramble to keep up. Life less resembles a fire drill for us now; we are getting more sleep, but it remains a constant challenge. Every day we find new reasons to realize that the early years actually were the easy ones. Occasionally, we find subjects besides the children to talk about.

My children cannot yet read about themselves. When they can, I hope they will not see this book as an invasion of their privacy, but rather as an unvarnished and loving memoir of the way we were. I am bad at baby books. When I am a grandmother, here is something I can give to my children. Then they will understand how life recycles itself.

These essays will disappoint those seeking solutions or answers. I claim to have none. But I hope this book offers entertainment and comfort to any mother whose children cannot believe she was ever a little girl. It is dedicated to all parents who have learned to tell time by cartoon shows and who have ever found footprints inside their refrigerators. We are all in this together.

As a family, mine is like many others. My book is a celebration of the ordinary and the shared experience. It was written the way parents will read it: while the washing machine is running, during nap times, and after everyone is asleep.

Writing this book has allowed me to step back and apply perspective to the closeness of daily life. It has given me the breathing space to laugh. Writing this book has led me to impose an illusion of order upon the chaos of years that are filled with mindless tasks and trying times. Writing reminds me these years also are filled with discovery and love.

Three years ago when I began to write about my family, I wondered if I would exhaust my material and run out of things to say. I need not have worried.

Acknowledgments

My writing is born out of a need to express my thoughts, but friends and colleagues have helped me to clarify them along the way.

I want to thank friends and neighbors, especially other mothers, whose long conversations and living illustrations have contributed greatly to these essays. I also owe a debt to all the women over the years who, with love, have watched my children when I could not.

My agent, Carla Mayer Glasser, believed in me when I was not sure. And Nancy Miller, my editor at Addison-Wesley, frequently helped me to see what I was trying to say. They both took a chance on me.

The columns upon which this book is based began in the *Orange County Register* in March of 1987. I have grown greatly on the job. Richard Cheverton, my editor, has never failed to support me. I'm grateful for his confidence.

And, finally, I want to thank the many women who have taken the time to write me. They have taught me two things: I am not alone—and this, too, shall pass.

Husband Is the Past Tense of Daddy

☙

1

Coping When Those Around You Have Given Up

V ERY clearly I remember the morning we brought our first baby home from the hospital. I reposed in the wheelchair outside the lobby, while my husband did battle with the car seat. Like many new parents, we took seriously the labels we read on much of our newly purchased baby gear. So when the car seat advertised it served bodies ranging in size from newborn to 40 pounds, we believed it. My husband fought with the tentacles of the straps, and I fought an unfriendly urge to ask him why he hadn't installed the apparatus the night before. I also fought the dawning revelation that the baby would have to be glued into place in order for the seat to fit properly.

Just then a childbirth instructor paraded by her class on its way to view the nursery. As she passed us, she told her students: "Don't be like that couple and wait until the last minute to install the car seat. Try to be prepared."

My chagrin lingered for several weeks after that—weeks during which I tried to cope with a plethora of new equipment all deemed essential for the up-and-coming baby, but totally baffling to the down-and-out new mother. My husband braved assembling the crib and the swing. He had to. I am a college graduate, but I would have paid for a crib sheet on the instructions to the Aprica stroller. (For two weeks I didn't dare collapse it.)

Prepared? Nothing can prepare you for the skills you will need to be a mother. You have to learn them in the trenches of sleepless nights and long, napless afternoons.

My three-year-old daughter endlessly plays mommy with her stuffed animals. She covers them up and pounds them to sleep, and drags them about the house by their legs. She knows as much about mothering as I did. It actually is possible to come home from the hospital without ever having seen your baby unwrapped from the waist down. The first week home I was close to tears because fate had dealt me two jokers: not only a belly button to deal with, but a circumcision as well. I didn't expect the Gerber baby, but I wasn't prepared for ooze and blood. I had listened to the hospital baby bathing demonstration intently, but later I wished I had taken notes.

In the physical sense, a baby doesn't rely on adults for much. Just everything. A mother doesn't have to learn much. Just everything about what it takes to keep another human being alive.

To start with, nursing a newborn can be intimidating. I have never understood how learning to do what comes naturally can require so much training. Never have I sweated so much as the early days spent waving myself in front of my baby's mouth, trying to get him to the right place, and trying to make him open up sufficiently when he got there. When he finally latched on properly, then I faced a different dilemma. I knew it was time to interrupt and make him switch sides, but I didn't want to start the whole process over again. Once a baby learns how to nurse, however, he makes it appear effortless. How can it be work when it puts infants to sleep? Well, any sweaty mother who has tried to duplicate his efforts with a manual pump can tell you that it is.

Babies come with pint-sized tanks; they need fill-ups as often as any guzzler. So whenever you have a spare moment to sit, you automatically will know it's time to get up and feed your baby. After feeding, you must do two things: Go in quest of the big burp, and wait for the big poop. If one comes quickly, then it's axiomatic the other will take forever. Like children when company comes, babies never perform when you want them to. And woe to the mother who lays an infant down before both have been accomplished. She has set a ticking time bomb.

Three children later, I realize how adept I have become. A friend called four weeks after her first baby was born. She had three questions: Is it all right to take the baby out of the house yet? Do you put the baby into the Snugli before or after you strap it on? How many times a day do I have to bathe the baby?

I talked with another friend after the shower for her first baby. She stared in amazement at the equipment piled in her living room: a car seat, an infant car seat, a baby carrier, a baby swing, a backpack, and a Snugli. Overwhelmed, she asked: "Is there anything here I don't need?"

With a touch of pride I can boast I successfully have made the swing, the carrier, the playpen, the stroller, and the high chair "user friendly." Now not only can I collapse and reassemble a stroller one-handed in 30 seconds, but I can hoist a baby into a papoose unassisted, all while functioning on less than eight hours sleep and two or more interruptions per night.

But now, of course, I have packed most of that stuff away. I can view anything with nostalgia, once it's behind me. In time, even the hardware wars of the early days can look enjoyable. Now I realize that learning to use baby equipment turns out to be easier than learning to do without it. About the time a parent comes to rely on swings and seats, the child has outgrown their purpose. Your reaction to this is the same as the first time you put your baby down someplace and come back to find he has moved.

The whole process of growing up can be defined, in a very physical sense, as a matter of freedom and control. As your children grow up, they increase their share of freedom to move about. They also diminish your control to stop them.

At the beginning, thanks to all the baby gadgets, infants have very little freedom and parents have a great deal of control. Overwhelming at first, that equipment now represents a relatively simpler time. Some of my favorite times have been in the car, with all the kids securely buckled into place. Drive-up windows and drive-through restaurants acquire a whole new appeal. Not only do you know exactly where your kids are, but there is a brief moment after you deposit them in the car and close the doors on your way to the driver's side, when you also effectively have silenced them. Their screams and demands are as impotent as a commercial without volume. I walk very slowly.

Of course, some children attempt to assert their independence from mechanical devices. Many a baby perfects the so-called anti-car-seat posture in which the infant stiffens his body like a board. Others become experts at climbing: out of the stroller, out of the high chair, etc. At this point, however, you maintain the obvious advantage. You are bigger than they are. Even the anti-car-seat posture can be thwarted either by tickling a child's belly or by a karate chop to the back of the knees.

But for almost a year, your child pretty much stays where you put him. Unbeknownst at the time, some of your sweetest memories may be of the child sacked out in the stroller, snoozing in the backpack, or snuggled in the papoose. Safe, silent, and immobile.

The flip side, of course, is your children's coming of age: when the restraints come off. It begins subtly. First, you move the car seat from the front seat to the rear—a strategic error because after that everything goes on behind your back. Then, almost overnight, your youngster qualifies for a booster seat. Gradually, babies grow their way out of high chairs, swings, backpacks, and cribs.

The kids come of age; you simply age. Suddenly, the child who always sat still throughout dinner at the table in a high chair, is a veritable jumping-jack in and out of his big-boy chair. The angel once locked securely in her car seat, suddenly has access to the seat belt and the rest of the car from her booster seat. And the toddler who used to howl from the confines of the crib has graduated to an adult bed. He now suffers a magnetic attraction to your bed at night. You will know you have left behind the last vestige of physical control when you let your child out of the grocery cart and allow him to walk down the aisles in the store.

From then on, as far as I can see, it's a downhill slide. The kids get their freedom and you lose some of your control. Your time isn't your own when you constantly are chasing after the disappearing back of a child. Anxiety alone is enough to make you nostalgic for the days when they couldn't walk. It only gets worse. My three year old already thinks she is ready to play in front of the house by herself. It's only a matter of time before she wants to cross the street alone.

So far, I won't let her. I still watch when the five year old crosses. They do not seem old enough to me, but children have a habit of growing when their parents aren't looking. It seems that no sooner do you learn how to hold your baby properly,

when suddenly it's time to learn how to let go of your child—
another skill for which there is no training.

IN my household we call it flying without a net. I remember
when that figure of speech was born. One day my husband
took the baby over to the bed, laid him down atop the beige
bedspread, and proceeded to strip off his diaper. He hoisted
him into the air by his legs, much like a trussed turkey, and
then reached for the clean diaper.

I inquired: "Taking a bit of a risk, aren't you?"

"Yep," he smiled, this father of three. "I'm flying without a
net."

The expression refers to those risk-taking times when you
take a leap of faith and rely on self-propulsion to bring you to
a safe landing. The first time we went flying without a net, of
course, my husband and I didn't even realize we were airborne.
That was when we decided to have children. We didn't know
what we were getting into, and we've been relying on faith
ever since.

But more concrete examples come to mind. Flying without
a net is when you're going to feed the baby his strained carrots,
but decide to skip the bib this one time. Flying without a net
is when you take just a short trip to the bank and decide it's
not worth taking along the diaper bag. And flying without a
net is when you send the four year old out alone to bring in
the mail.

Obviously, the more children you have, the more inclined
to risk-taking you become. I know a woman with five children,
and she entrusts the nine year old with her baby when she
isn't even in the same room. In handling our third baby, my
husband and I seem like veritable daredevils in comparison to

how we cosseted our first. We let him go more places, eat new foods faster, and get dirtier than his siblings ever did.

But when it comes to the older children, the ones venturing into uncharted territory, I've noticed my feet are more likely to remain stuck on the ground.

For a long time I preferred to keep the telephone a mystery to my five year old son. I didn't want him playing with it and didn't want him to use it. But now at preschool he's learning how to dial for help in an emergency, and I realize I'm doing myself no favor by keeping him ignorant. The same thing with the key to the house. We keep it by the front door, up high where it cannot be played with and lost. But when the house is locked, the key is required in order to get out. If there were a fire, do I want my children locked inside?

It's like the safety latches we installed on all the cabinets. For years I was relieved to rely on them to keep little fingers away from the supplies inside. But my daughter figured them out when she was nearly three. And suddenly I have to rely on her good judgment and a measure of fear to keep her away from the shampoo or the cleaning supplies inside. Recognizing that the children are growing up, and then giving them the responsibilities that come along with it, is not easy. Learning to use the car seat was hard, but this is harder. It means relinquishing absolute control over their lives. It is flying without a net.

Even the baby was fast to get into the high-wire act. At eight months old, already he persisted in standing whenever possible—cruising his way around couches and chairs. He would balance upright, swaying, defying gravity for long seconds at a stretch before toppling. By nine months he was walking. Life was easier when he was content to crawl. Now he is climbing atop tables, and I worry he will fall and crash his head into sharp corners and onto hard floors. But I force myself to let go and allow him to learn. It's a skill I need to practice. I know parents can't keep children in playpens the rest of their lives.

ﻭﻭ

WHILE a parent can perfect many skills through practice, others are not improved with use. Patience is one of them. Your weekly visit to the grocery store, for example, can regularly put your patience to the test.

My daughter is heavy in my arms as we walk across the parking lot to the grocery store. My son, three years old and barely potty trained, is slow at my side as he balances on the curbs and jumps over cracks in the sidewalk.

Once inside, shortly after I load the cart with frozen foods, he clutches his pants in the universal distress signal and announces he has to go potty. So I try to amuse the toddler and convince her not to stand in the cart while we wait for him down one of those little hallways off the dairy case where the floor never is very clean. My son doesn't come out.

"He'll be out soon," says the stock boy who emerges first.

"Not done yet," yells my son after I pound on the door.

Emboldened eventually, I prop open the bathroom door—keeping my daughter within eyesight—and shout instructions from the doorway. He hobbles from the stall, angry, because he couldn't pull his pants up over the heels of his shoes. And the poop didn't come. It doesn't come after we dash from the produce section or after we leave our place in the check-out line, either. Finally, we make it home where everything works out fine, and I have kept my patience about something over which he had no control.

But after we are home, I lose it. The 15 month old is taking food out of the grocery bags far faster than I can put it away, and she drops a can on my shoe. I'm wearing sandals.

"What was in the can?" my son inquires sweetly, after I finish screaming.

Patience is a precious commodity that parents must mine regularly. It's the resource you dredge up when anger isn't appropriate or won't be effective. It's a skill mandatory for the job.

Children try your patience in one of two ways: either on purpose or without realizing it. The most notorious example of a child's deliberate assault is the temper tantrum. Advising a parent how to cope with a temper tantrum is a bit like a man advising a woman about labor pains. You have to earn your stripes. So first, let me establish my credentials as a mother who had a two year old who orchestrated his furies like a virtuoso.

To me, the severity of a tantrum is not determined solely by the volume of screams. Many children can shriek and scream words unintelligible except for their aggrieved tone. No, a superior tantrum also must include red or even blue faces—although not necessarily a trace of tears. It also requires flailing limbs that turn a child into a lethal windmill. Lastly, a world-class tantrum is a function of location: It has left the privacy of your home and entered a public place where embarrassment comes into play. If you cannot make yourself heard to a child, and if you risk bodily harm to touch him, then he has mastered a tantrum worthy of contention.

The proper way to respond to a tantrum, the "experts" agree, is not to throw one yourself. Simply remain cool and detached. That's easy to do if you aren't angry. It's also easy if the screaming child is not your own or if you truthfully don't care (at least for the moment) whether he survives to become a responsible adult.

One time-honored strategy is to leave the child and walk away. His performance is meaningless without an audience.

My children, recognizing this, have never been too proud to follow me—screaming—from room to room. Another strategy is to exile the child to his room, not to emerge until he can behave. The drawback to this technique of "time out" is that it may require throwing repeated body blocks against the bedroom door to imprison the offender inside. Another mother swears by shock treatment: dousing a screamer's head with cold water to startle him into breaking his momentum. Good strategies all, but useless against a world-class screamer.

I can remember one time we were seeing Daddy off at the airport, standing at the boarding gate, when for reasons obscure even then, my son went into his act. Right there, on the floor of the exit, he was a pugnacious boulder trying to dam the flow of the crowd. Words were useless to budge him. Fortunately, I have perfected a variation of a half-Nelson hold in which I grasp a screaming child the length of his torso, arms and legs pointed away from me, balance his weight against my hip, and carry him. We managed to get out of the way of less-than-sympathetic boarding passengers, but we couldn't get as far as the parking lot. I deposited him on a street corner outside the terminal.

"Look at the little boy crying," a mother said to her little girl crouched in front of my son. "Maybe he'd like to play with you, Sara," she said—no doubt trying to be helpful and distract him. But he didn't want to play, obviously, and she should have known it. Now other mothers may disagree, but I prefer strangers to stay out of it. He started it with me and he's going to have to settle it with me. I didn't want to have to apologize when he started screaming at her, too, just as I didn't want to have to worry about what harm he might inflict on the stewardess who offered to carry him to our car.

In the end, I waited him out with what I believe was saintlike patience. His battery ran down, we made it home, and he lived to turn three. In retrospect, maybe he was smarter than I realized. Parents can sit out a Grade A tantrum, but they can't stop it. Maybe that's why kids throw them; they know sometimes it can put them in control. They also know most parents don't throw temper tantrums of their own in front of witnesses.

Although I shouldn't, I do lose my patience and throw the adult version of a tantrum. Contrary to all advice and my own intentions, I shout and scream when I have reached the breaking point. Unlike my children, however, I wait until we are in the privacy of our home. In an emergency, I pinch in public. Most onlookers can't see it, but the kids can feel it.

Most often, of course, I try to be patient—particularly when my kids don't mean to be bad, but somehow their behavior is as tedious as making a freeway interchange during rush-hour traffic.

Like a traffic jam, children change the tempo of life. Everything about them takes longer. They walk slower and respond slower—but expect you to do just the opposite when fetching them refills on juice or finding time to read them a book. The sheer logistics of hauling three kids and dry-cleaning in and out of the car can be overwhelming. You wouldn't want to take them all inside the bank on the same day you go to the cleaners. That would be (pardon the pun) pressing your luck. It's like walking with your shoelaces tied to somebody else's shoes. With coordination you can get there from here, but not very quickly.

I keep reminding myself that there are advantages to slowing down and taking a walk with someone who studies the cracks in the sidewalk. The idea is not to get somewhere in a hurry, but to enjoy going nowhere slowly. Sometimes, by growing up, we outgrow the ability to relax and enjoy. Children can teach us to remember to play and to smell the flowers. They teach us to grow down. When confronted by two children who would rather chase each other around the bedroom than get into the car, you have two choices. If I have the time, I know it can be better to run around in circles screaming with them, than to stand on the sidelines screaming at them.

Patience, in short, is what you need the day the toddler discovers the volume control on the television set, or she runs around the house shutting all the doors—but hasn't a clue how to get them open. Patience is what you need when the kids sneak talcum powder downstairs to make it snow all over themselves and the carpeting. It's what you need when you discover they are making water balloons in the bathroom. And it helps you deal with a child whose idea of an insult is to call you a pooh-pooh ca-ca.

Your children are oblivious to all the ways in which they try your patience. One of the biggest ways they annoy is by treating their parents like radio interference. They simply tune us out.

One day my children were playing outside with the boys next door. Covered in dirt, they all began edging inside toward my neighbor's kitchen.

"We don't want them going inside, do we?" I asked her.

"Hey!" she called from the end of the driveway. "Come back outside."

"Stay outside," I echoed. The response was underwhelming.

"Notice how nobody is moving," I commented, deferring to her proprietorship since it was her garage. She had first rights on screaming.

"Now!" she barked, and the troops did an about-face.

The response time, she opined, is directly proportionate to the volume of the shout. This is so, I believe, because children's ears break. Somewhere between the ages of two-and-one-half and three, the body part simply wears out. The connection between the ear and the brain must disintegrate, making contact intermittent. And unless the auditory impulse is reinforced by the visual—i.e., you force the kid to look at you when you're talking—they don't hear.

Lives there a mother so perfect she never has shouted at her offspring: "Listen to me (shake, shake) when I'm talking to you!" One father calls it "selective deafness." One mother has a standing rule: She repeats nothing more than twice, regardless of what catastrophe results. Yes, children's ears break; mommies' aren't allowed to. But when a mom wears out, her patience can be the first thing to go.

2 The Family Numbers Game

WHEN my neighbor's freezer stopped working, she brought all her food over to my house—including her midnight snacks. Late one night, with some embarrassment, she crept into my kitchen to retrieve her pint of ice cream.

Because it was one of those new flavors I had never tried, the next day I asked her if it was good.

"Not as good as I thought it would be, but I couldn't stop eating it," she admitted.

Having children, I believe, is a lot like eating ice cream. On a day-to-day basis it isn't always as good as we thought it would be—but that doesn't seem to stop us from having more.

Deciding to have a child is taking a leap of faith into the pool of life. Despite the overwhelming evidence of logic against it, somehow you assume you will stay afloat. But nobody teaches you how; you may drown in your own good intentions.

Parenting offers rewards and extracts a price you never can fully anticipate. Nobody can give you an appraisal of what it will cost. You realize ahead of time, for example, that you have decided to dedicate your life to your children. But did you also realize you have sacrificed your furniture and your carpeting?

Becoming a parent is like taking the vows of poverty and chastity: The children come first. Children are expensive. Do not be surprised when yours are better dressed then you. They are showered with stylish gifts at birth and require new wardrobes with every season because nothing fits. (Later, this gives them practice for when the clothes fit but nothing is in style.) Likewise, your child will make more trips to the doctor in the first two years of his life than you have taken in your last 20. He will be treated for every ailment; you will see no one as you struggle to get over those same ailments that you catch from him.

Children also cost a lot in terms of attention. You spend most of your time on them, leaving little for you or for your husband. When you do have a private moment, you're most likely to spend it in the bathroom. On a quiet afternoon you'll find yourself craving a nap. "Privacy" is a noun; it cannot be conjugated from "parent."

Despite the drawbacks, however, each year millions of women cast aside inexperience, fears, and all the dictates of logic by becoming mothers. Then, after the fact, we often are reminded forcibly that there is no way of knowing how our children will turn out. Yes, we will love them—but will we like them?

If kids were mufflers, they would come with guarantees. They would be healthy, smart, attractive, and well behaved. Most, of course, would violate the warranty. Muffled does not apply to children whose speaking voices can shatter eardrums and peace of mind. Even if we kept the receipt, who on earth would take them back? The sniffling kid, the snotty kid wiping his nose on his shirt sleeve belongs to you. That child screaming hysterically for a helium balloon priced at $6.99 belongs to you. And the barbarian who has just bitten the child next door during an all-out war over a stick is yours.

Deciding to have a child, in short, is at once the smartest and the dumbest thing you can do. You almost certainly will never regret it; you almost certainly will be sorry. What can you say about an undertaking that saps your time, energy, pocketbook, and marriage? It would not survive spread-sheet analysis.

Having said all that about a first child, why would anyone have a second? A parent has to wonder: Do you love harder with more kids, or can it be harder to love?

A child, of course, is a wondrous thing. From his eyes that look like yours, to his nose that looks like your husband's, reproduction is a miracle. So is the growth that follows. Your child learns to walk and talk; you learn new facets of love. Your child learns to hit and grab; you learn new forms of patience. Each day one child all by himself can be a complete challenge, totally absorbing. So it's understandable that many parents—already giving their all and wanting it to be their best—drop out of the childbearing derby. No more laps around the field for them.

Before I had my second child and especially my third, I couldn't understand the only-child logic. An only child, I thought, was a third wheel, part of an unmatched set. My family would be a wagon, not a wheelbarrow. But hindsight forces me to admit that the form of a wheelbarrow perfectly follows its function. If children are aggravation, then why ask for more? If children always demand more time, energy, and patience than you can deliver, why multiply the requests?

Like a faraway oasis, the thought of hearing only one voice at a time talking in my ears is tantalizing. But for me it is only a mirage. Sometimes I feel like I work behind the counter of a bakery. Mentally, I am always giving my children numbers so I know who comes next. If I had one child, instead of always taking turns, instead of always having to share, that child could have my complete attention.

I can see the advantages. Everything he did would be new; I would never have seen it before. One child goes through each stage only once. The training pants in my household would have been relegated to dust rags by now. Without siblings, there can be no rivalry. Without younger siblings, an only child gets to go places sooner. My five year old has not yet made it to the museum because the three year old isn't mature enough.

So if there's something to be said for never starting, there's even more to be said for stopping after one. Except, of course, that some of us don't—stop, that is. Maybe we want the girl or the boy we didn't get the first time; maybe we want to avert a lonely childhood; maybe we just love children. Or maybe we are asking for trouble. One mother told me: "I already have the perfect child. Why should I have another?" Now I know you don't have a second child to see if it will be better, but to see how it will be different.

The point is, some time after your child turns one and before he hits six, you are faced with a choice: Buy him a dog or have another baby. A certifiable number of women opt for the baby.

If you opt for the baby, then you have to decide when—or rather, how soon. Which raises another perplexing issue: When it comes to spacing out children, must you decide how close together or how far apart? Wait too long and life starts to become comfortable. Wait too little and while the children may grow up to be fast friends, you might not survive to see it.

I still can remember a mother I once saw at the park. Pushing her one-year-old daughter, she was something of a natural wonder. She was nine months pregnant.

Awestruck, we other ladies sneaked glances at the bulging belly she carried and then at the toddler she pushed. "She isn't adopted," someone whispered. Then we rolled our eyes toward heaven and marveled. I cannot decide whether we were more impressed that she managed to get pregnant again so quickly— or that she looked so happy about it.

Some mothers, I understand, get pregnant even more quickly. Resuming conjugal relations, they jump the gun on the doctor-prescribed six-week recovery period after having a baby. Six weeks may constitute proper recovery clinically speaking, but emotionally speaking it takes me more than a year to feel anything like normal. I know this is so because just like clockwork my children have arrived 25 months after their predecessors. Women who jump the gun make mockery of the adage: One child trained on the potty is worth two in diapers. Such mothers don't have to worry about postponing potty training because of a new arrival, however. It's too early to even start.

What I can't figure out is which schedule is best. Do you want to grow your children like a crop or nurture them one seedling at a time?

My children are fairly close together. Theoretically, once they stop competing they will grow up to be great friends. Certainly they never will be able to say, "Oh, my brother, he was so much older, I never knew him very well." I see other virtues in harvesting a bumper crop. Once you are immersed in diapers and bottles already, for example, why not stay there? If you wait to have children four years apart, you've just returned to normal before starting all over again. With close kids, for brief periods of time their interests actually overlap. You can save money by buying the same toy for both kids—and then you can teach them to share it.

The women who beat the clock amaze me, but so do the women who slow it down. They aren't conned by the innocence of babies. Babies beguile you with their sweetness so you want more. Then, when you are committed and six months pregnant again, your first child hits the Terrible Twos. Too late.

Considerations cut both ways. If you have your babies close together, then they aren't old enough to remember solitude and you won't have any. If you wait until your eldest is already in school, then while he is gone you can pretend the next child is an only child. But your child-bearing years easily can consume a decade.

I blame birth control for the whole dilemma. Ever since it put the "planning" in "family," many women have been able to order up their babies, give or take a month, on the schedule they desire. But I have to wonder if the planning has gone too far. Sure, I'm familiar with postponing children until you are financially secure. But one woman told me she wants to plan her second pregnancy around her child's preschool vacation. And I read about a pregnant law school student who planned to deliver her baby after finals, study for the bar while she recovered, and then start her job in the fall.

I must confess, I had my children the old-fashioned way— without having the slightest clue how we would earn enough to support them. On the other hand, maybe those other women are smarter. An accountant's daughter, I delivered babies in January and February—just in time to miss a whole year's tax deduction for each.

But if the issue is timing when you have a second child, it is not with the third. The issue becomes justification. Because while nobody will quarrel with your decision to have a second child, many people look askance at you for having a third.

The difference becomes apparent during pregnancy. The first time, excitement overrides all reason; you are awed by and proud of your enlarging belly. The second time around, you're more matter of fact as practical concerns take precedence. You know what to expect and spend a lot of time trying to convey it in positive terms to your firstborn. But by the third pregnancy you are, like your stomach muscles, a little less resilient. Instead of accepting congratulations, you find yourself fielding questions. People want to know why you did it again—particularly when you said you never would. Up until the birth of my third child, I still hadn't formulated an adequate response. (Should I have a fourth child, I suspect people would stop asking.)

When I was pregnant with number three, my son broke the news to his grandfather. "Is he kidding?" my father asked. The other side of the family wasn't much more positive. "You're brave," my mother-in-law said. Foolhardy, I think, might be a more accurate description.

Everyone knows the "perfect" all-American family consists of Mommy, Daddy, and two children, a boy and a girl. I already had that. The world is engineered for a family of four. Cars seat four, houses comfortably sleep four. We have two hands, one for grabbing the collar of each kid. And each child has two parents. That way he can always get the attention of at least one of them.

While I was pregnant, I found it hard to imagine myself as the mother in a family of five. I was hard pressed to manage my family of four. With one child I had his immunization record memorized; with two children I could not remember to schedule their checkups. In the summer I barely found time to nurture the garden. I found myself vaguely annoyed that the flowers weren't big enough to water themselves. I know that family multiplication tables defy the laws of mathematics. They say having two children is more than twice as much as having one. Where would that leave three? Three kids, I decided, must be like juggling. You just keep one child up in the air at all times. That is, of course, one of those feats that looks easier when somebody else is doing it.

Despite my misgivings, I remember giving pep talks to my children, particularly my son. I waxed poetic about how marvelous a new baby would be. But my son, like me, harbored no illusions.

"Won't another baby be a lot of trouble?" Those were the first words out of his mouth upon hearing the news. "Is this baby going to sit on the drain in the bathtub?" he wanted to know. "That's the only place left." Then, after pondering a while, he informed me I couldn't have another boy because that would mean I'd have two.

That is, of course, another argument against three. Once you already have a boy and a girl, anything new constitutes duplication. And in the childbearing derby, I was an easy winner. In two tries, I had one of each sex. I can gloat when I hear about the woman who cried when she delivered her fifth baby and her fifth boy. As I said, children are like ice cream: Most parents want to sample chocolate and vanilla.

Now that I have my three children, I realize it is not that simple. No two are alike. They come in a variety of flavors and offer a bounty of opportunities. It's like living in the desert but within driving distance of the mountains. I can enjoy infinite variety all in the same family. Kids to the power of three equals more hugs, more kisses, and more loving.

But just as deciding to start a family is a momentous decision, so is deciding to stop. My husband and I dove unprepared into parenting, yet so far we are keeping our heads above water. I do, however, see warning signs. Kids to the power of three also equals more noise, more commotion, and more stress. I've discovered I don't enjoy the company of my three each day nearly so much after the first 12 hours. And, some days, I love them best when they are all asleep.

When it comes to having more children, I think it's time for me to stop. The other morning I left them all peacefully upstairs while I went outside to get the newspaper. Moments later the crescendo of their screams, pouring out the open window, shattered the early morning peace. I had this tremendous urge to wrap my bathrobe tightly about me, muster my dignity while I still could, and just keep on going.

MOTHERS of only one, perched on the child-bearing fence and considering carefully whether they wanted to jump again, used to ask me what it was like to have two. Different, I used to answer.

I can remember taking my first baby on his newborn visit to the pediatrician. Not knowing what emergency might arise, I carried a diaper bag into which I crammed extra diapers, powder, ointment, puddle pad, plastic bags, wipes, washcloth, pacifier, toy, sweater, hat, undershirt, and a change of clothes. Two years later, taking my second newborn on her first trip, I carried my purse.

For the second born, position in life explains the baby book stuffed with mementos to be organized another day. It's the reason a child not yet two knows all about cookies and ice cream, whereas an older sibling at that age never knew they existed. For years my eldest never knew restaurants served hamburgers on buns with french fries and ketchup. My daughter does.

Position in life explains the smile that has acquired a mouthful of teeth between photographs, and it explains why the knees of the coveralls are dirty when the baby isn't yet crawling. The second born isn't the first to wear those clothes. Likewise, she isn't the first to walk, and sometimes she can be the last to claim your undivided attention.

With a second child, your standards change; some would say they slide. A mother who sterilized a pacifier dropped by a first child, only rinses it for the second. If once she changed the entire outfit when a diaper leaked, the second time she may only make sure the dampness doesn't touch skin. The second baby doesn't get to go to mommy-and-me exercise classes. From the very first day, it's mommy and us. Nor does she get to be rocked long after she's asleep just because it feels cozy to cuddle her inside a quiet house.

Experienced parents take some experiences for granted. I remember that I used to watch my firstborn sleep. I also crawled in order to demonstrate to him the mechanics when he wasn't getting the hang of it. The second child learned without assistance. Likewise, the second time around I wasn't surprised when my child wanted to play in the toilet bowl, parade through the house naked, or eat sand.

So the second child grows up differently. She knows she's not the first; Kilroy is always one step ahead of her. The second child has someone to copy, someone to be compared to, and someone to compete against. My firstborn's first word was "Da Da." I don't remember for the second—except that she quickly learned to say "mine," delivered in a screech. She talked and walked sooner, already engaged in her life-long effort to catch up.

As a parent, certainly you are more at ease with, but less all-consumed by, a second child. I went into labor worrying about how my oldest would accept his sibling; I came home from the hospital trying to pretend that although I had had a baby, nothing had really changed. After my first child was born, I remember a succession of bathrobe days in which the baby and I hibernated inside. I thought managing to cook dinner was an accomplishment. After my second child was born, I can remember taking both kids to the park within a week because I couldn't stand to be cooped up in the house any longer.

The father who once gingerly cradled a baby with hands made clumsy by awe, the second time knows he can toss an infant high into the air to elicit belly laughs. The gadgets that can so paralyze a new mother hardly faze her the second time around. With one hand she can collapse the stroller, install the car seat, and assemble the food grinder without reading directions. And she wonders why she thought she was overwhelmed after her first child was born.

My second time, in short, I thought I coped fairly well—far better than I had the first. It required three children to teach me humility.

As the mother of three, my powers of concentration are shot. Twice now I have run downstairs, turned on the oven, and come back later only to find I forgot also to put the dinner inside. After 5 P.M., when the children all get hungry, cranky, tired, and try to talk at once, is like the downside of a roller coaster ride. I just pick up momentum until everyone lands in bed.

Three, I learned in school, is greater than two. But before, I never fully realized the implications. Three can make more noise. One day, as we worked our way through Sesame Street,

Play Dough, and story hour, I spoke to one adult the entire time: the librarian who checked out our books—and I couldn't hear what she said; the baby was screaming in my ear while the other two argued. When I took all three to the pediatrician's for checkups, their commotion rattled the entire staff. One nurse forced my daughter to stop making soap bubbles in the sink. Another, awed perhaps by the number of naked bodies, pitched in to help get them dressed. Then she forgot to administer the shot she came in for.

Hanging onto three kids requires practicing crowd control. Crossing the street, holding the toddler in one arm, it's a lot more difficult to keep everyone moving together because one child has no hand to hold. I find myself trying to compensate with volume for what I lack in direct physical control. I take constant mental roll call as my eyes dart in rotation from child to child.

Three kids means more of everything. The only appliance on more than the television set is the washing machine. It's serious strategy whether to do one manageable load per day, or tackle the Himalayas once a week. Likewise, it is not a casual decision to cut 30 fingernails at one sitting—60 if you want to argue over toes.

The viewing public responds to the family of five in one of two ways: disbelief or sympathy. Some strangers who admire the baby visibly shudder when they realize the other two also belong with me. They exchange discreetly appalled looks as if we are Third World specimens to be viewed only on the pages of National Geographic. Women with more than two of their own merely offer co-conspiratorial grins and help by holding open the door. Other mothers are overwhelmed. I babysat one day for my son's playmate when his mother was in a jam. She thanked me profusely and offered to return the favor. "I'll take your son," she said, "if you have to go somewhere." She paused. "I'll even take your daughter," she added. But she trailed off into silence as she realized there was still the toddler.

All of which is the best way I can answer mothers of merely one or two who want to know what it's like to have three kids. I also asked that question once—and now I can appreciate why that other mother didn't have a chance to answer.

3 Will the Real Mother Please Stand Up?

MY son, the child-care worker informed me, needed to learn who was boss.

"He's expecting somebody to come running every time he cries," she said. "You need to be more firm with him."

Foolish, first-time mother, I listened to her. It took me a while to realize she was not trying to help me be a better mother, but to make her job easier. When you first become a parent, you're not sure about anything—so you think everyone else is.

The biological fact of giving birth automatically makes you a mother, just as a driver's license allows you to drive. But you become comfortable behind the wheel only through a combination of experience and aggravation—the same way you earn the title of mother.

Your baby, who knows nothing and has no expectations, accepts you as his authority. He may not recognize your inexperience, but inside you are well aware of it. Subconsciously you wait for the real mother to take charge, even though your hands are shaking because your mind insists that it must be you.

That inner uncertainty can persist. Five years after the fact, I still don't always feel like a full-fledged mother. Mother's Day

27

cards are something I mail out, not something I receive. Other mothers always seem more confident in their roles than I am— particularly those with older children. Once you have gone beyond the pale of home and conquered kindergarten, for example, you're close to earning a black belt in parenting. Those mothers seem to have their acts together; mine feels like improvisation all the way.

There are signs—emotional white hairs—that signal a woman's conversion into a mother. They are changes you feel on the inside and changes in how others see you on the outside. Eventually, there are changes in the way you act. No longer an understudy, you begin to act the part.

Within the privacy of my own home, I am starting to realize how far I have come. Out of the corner of my eye I catch glimpses in the mirror of some mother hugging her son, and vaguely it registers that the mother is me. My mental Rolodex has expanded beyond addresses and telephone numbers and the birthdays on my husband's side of the family. Now it includes the shoe sizes of my three children, which of them hates tomatoes, and if they liked the flavor of the most recent antibiotic they took. Sometimes I listen to myself issuing instructions and I marvel inwardly that the seemingly self-assured voice is mine. Who taught me to assert with such authority that only three crackers are allowed for after-school snack?

When it comes to accepting advice, I now consider the source. I was seriously rattled by that child-care provider, who had no children of her own. She has since had a baby, and I'd like to advise her to let him scream. For several days I listened to another mother, who bottle-fed her babies, as she advised me not to nurse my infant until the clock said he was hungry.

Once I sat in a restaurant with my son when his allergies

began acting up. He deals with this through a series of prolonged, wrenching coughs. No fewer than five people stopped by our table to point out that he could be choking. They assumed, evidently, I hadn't noticed.

Have you canceled your subscriptions to parenting magazines that feature 10 tips for avoiding sunburn? Have you been downright annoyed by the stranger in the checkout line who offers advice on how to cope with your screaming infant while you try to write a check? Then you're starting to feel like an experienced mother. Advice, you've decided, is not like money. You won't necessarily take it where you can get it.

Most advice is free, and once you become a parent, everyone will want to give it to you. In the beginning, like a panhandler, you had your hand out to take anything.

The first-time parents, who still believe events having to do with children can be described in rational terms, rush immediately from the obstetrician's office to the library. I have my doubts all that reading helps. I read, for example, the layette list published by the baby clothing manufacturers and took it all literally. To this day there are items I have never used. The first thing I wanted to throw at my husband during the transition phase of labor was the preparation booklet from the childbirth class. His reading about how I was feeling didn't help, any more than when he told me my eyes were wandering from my focal point. Once the baby came home, I used to compare his development to the chapters in the books. I stopped after several months, after realizing that the child in the book and the child in my nursery bore no relationship to each other.

Real mothers become picky about taking advice. I like to cruise my local playground. It's the social equivalent of a bathhouse, where you can engage in lots of casual, anonymous conversations with mothers who will confide endless details of their lives and how they cope. In the school of practical experience, these mothers have earned postdoctorate degrees. Authoritatively they can tell you the disadvantages of bottle liners or the advantages of snap-crotch undershirts. Because they don't know you, they have no vested interest in whether you do it their way.

As a mindset, however, motherhood means more than acquiring confidence in yourself, or even being able to understand a two year old whose speech is unintelligible to anyone without children.

You are a full-fledged mother when your kid throws a tantrum in public and—not only don't you give in—but you no longer are embarrassed. You have grown a thick skin. In addition to strangers who act as if you have no brains, you become used to children who act as if you have no feelings. Children believe their parents have all the emotional needs of cardboard. They are faster to verbalize their anger than their happiness.

"I want Daddy!" my daughter screams after I force her out of the bathtub. "I don't want you!"

"You never give me anything. I don't want to be with you," my son shouts after I deny him a fifth cookie.

As a mother you start to accept the notion that your child is not going to like you all of the time—and vice versa. As a mother you grow into your role as an authority figure.

I remember some years ago when my two children and my neighbor's were playing outside together on the far side of the bushes. Suddenly they came running toward us, crying and wet. Some big boys riding past on bicycles had clobbered them with water balloons. I knelt down to dispense comfort and kisses—but the other mother took off like a shot. A few minutes later she returned, panting.

"I caught up with them," she announced with a touch of pride. "I told them that wasn't a nice thing to do. They wouldn't like it if somebody hit them, and it isn't fair to pick on little kids."

"How old were the boys?" I asked.

"Ten or eleven," she answered. "But one of them actually apologized."

My neighbor, who has three years' seniority on me in this motherhood business, never hesitated before running after the meanies. New in my motherhood role, I never considered it.

Being a mother requires exerting authority over children. Right now this means being able to keep yours from playing in the street or eating graham crackers before dinner. It also means intervening when you see a strange two year old feeding his face with dirt, instead of waiting for his mother to surface. And if a child runs out in front of your car, you feel called upon to stop and give him a talk about safety, instead of just honking and driving away. When the occasions arise, I hope this also means I will be able to take charge during a medical emergency, argue with the principal when my child has been wronged, shout down a noisy Cub Scout troop, and get everyone back on the bus after visiting Disneyland.

While it's tough to say no to your own child, it's tougher to say no to somebody else's. Once you muster your inner fortitude to assert yourself, you can tell you have arrived if the kid obeys you. Subconsciously, I keep waiting for the retort: "You can't tell me what to do." But it never comes, so I must be learning the part. Instead of rebellion, I get the closed face and resigned sighs the kids probably give their own mothers.

As a mother, you are trying to restore a sense of order to your life. That is why in addition to giving your children love, you must also give them orders. Authority and discipline are tools mothers use in their struggle to regain control of life.

Before we had children, life for many of us was as well
ordered as the matched pumps lined up neatly inside the closet.
Our biggest indiscretions were leaving the dinner dishes overnight in the sink or lolling about Sunday mornings trailing
newsprint across the house. But we always knew that by Monday morning we would clean it up and restore order. Children
deny you that symmetry—in your life and inside your closet.
They mess up your plans the way they mess up your shoes.
They rarely finish what they start, and they start a lot of messes
you don't want to finish.

But you do. Like minnows swimming upstream, we mothers
are doomed to strive to create order out of chaos. Like children
who believe in magic, we believe if we try hard enough, surely
we can get caught up and finally get ahead. This attitude is a
leftover from the office, when hard work brought its own
rewards. Those were the days when a boss might compliment
for a job well done, and a paycheck every week was the world's
way of saying you did worthwhile work. We know raising
children is worthwhile work, but there are few compliments
for a job well done. Nobody says, "Neatly changed diaper."
Nobody says, "You displayed fine management skills coping
with six children from four families arguing over three video
games."

The mentality, however, lingers. So we repeat the same
chores day after day, hoping to shine, even though we merely
are running in place. It reminds me of the refrigerator door in
my kitchen. You give it a push toward closing, it swings and
then stalls inches away from sealing shut. No matter how many
times sticky hands pull the door open, a mother's role is to
make sure each time it finally closes.

In assigning ourselves this thankless task of being the responsible party, we women set ourselves up as nags and invite
our own aggravation. I cannot say for sure when my role as a

mother became intertwined with my function as a policeman. Maybe it began when the children started to explore the world. They did so by making messes.

When my toddler tears the checks out of my checkbook, he is practicing small motor coordination. When my five year old pours glue over the newspaper, he calls it art. When my three year old climbs up the refrigerator shelves, she learns spatial relationships.

As my children learned to make messes, I learned to clean them up. As a mother, my earliest role was picking up after them. Later it became forcing them to pick up after themselves. Somewhere along the line, I decided mess prevention was the shortest distance between their desires and my sanity. I began to try to head them off at the pass.

"Can we jump on your bed?"

"No, I just fixed the bedspread."

"Can we buy crayons for drawing in the bathroom?"

"No, they'll just make a mess all over the walls."

"Can we make a fort out of the couch?"

"No, you never pick up the cushions."

When I was a child, we had a name for somebody like me. We called such people party-poopers. And so I realize I have crossed the great divide. Instead of letting good times ignite, I dampen spirits.

Thus, I have started to act like the mother my children believe me to be. I make the beds and the rules. My husband may weigh more, but in my quest to assert control, I have become the heavy. I have come to believe rules are the dikes that stand between my family and the raging tide of barbarism. I erect them at the slightest provocation.

One morning, for example, even from upstairs I could hear my husband yelling at our daughter for coloring on the door.

"We only color on paper," he shouted, as if the problem were her hearing instead of her comprehension.

"No," I corrected him later in private. "The rule is that we only color on paper at the kitchen table; never in the den. She knows that's the rule; you ought to know it, too." He glared at me, wondering no doubt how he ended up being the one in trouble.

It all comes down to rules. Rules. I live my life by 'em. Posture may be what separates the man from the baboon. A man walks upright. But rules are what separate the child from the baboon, even if the child is still crawling. Rules take the jungle out of the child.

As a new mother, I was hesitant to impose rules on my children. I was fearful of making their childhood seem like one long exercise in applying for permission. So when my son was given a gigantic fire engine by his great-grandmother, I let him ride it in the house. I let him ride it outside. I let him park it in the kitchen. Finally, that toy was underfoot more than the floor. Then, one fateful day, as the fender rammed my ankle bone one time too many, I made up a rule. The fire engine, I pronounced, is an Outside Toy. And that is how it began.

We now have Inside Toys and Outside Toys, and I classify them before the wrapper hits the garbage: "No, sidewalk chalk cannot be tested on the carpet." "No, we cannot practice baseball in the family room." Thus, when the kids wanted to take the sheets off my bed to hang on a fort outside, all I had to do was say: "Stop. Those are Inside Only." No further explanation was necessary.

Rules have civilized us; they have created order out of chaos. I am Ayatollah the Mommy; my rulings come swift and merciless. And, I have learned to make them come at the beginning. Bargain while you still have leverage, I always say. After you give them the ice cream is no time to inform them that they can eat it only at the table. We used to walk all over the house eating and drinking. The carpet in front of the television set began to look like a picnic area after Memorial Day. Thus originated another rule: food and drink only in the kitchen or at the table. The only exception has been food that doesn't make crumbs. Apples, consequently, have enjoyed an amazing resurgence in popularity.

New situations, of course, demand improvisation. There was, for example, the magic moment when my son, then four, announced he had temporarily misplaced his chewing gum inside the car. Instant rule: No chewing gum inside the house or car. We have the if-you-take-out-a-toy rule. If you take it out, you must put it away before you get another one. A rebellious response to that rule produced another new rule: If Mommy puts it away, she gets to put it up high where you cannot reach it again.

Although it goes without saying, let me say that one of the biggest rules all mothers follow is always to respect the rule of another mother. This means if her child is allowed to run unescorted across the street while he eats tooth-rotting candy right before dinner, who am I to say otherwise? Mothers' emotional currency is backed by faith. Mutual respect keeps the system from collapsing.

Some psychologists say children are more comfortable with rules, anyway. They say they feel some relief in knowing their limits. I cannot vouch for how the children feel, but I know I feel some relief in setting their limits. I revel in each edict, drunk with my own authority. Some people lay carpet for a living; I lay down rules. You name it, I cover it: toys, bedtime, eating, and manners. And I will continue laying down rules, awaiting the inevitable day when my children will try to walk all over them.

That my children haven't revolted so far is an indication of how thoroughly I have adopted my role. As a mother, I am learning to keep my inner uncertainties to myself. I give a convincing performance. After five years, issuing orders finally seems to almost come naturally.

"Put your shoes away in the closet," I command on my first pass through the bedroom.

"In your closet, not under the table," I intone my second time around.

My son squares his shoulders resignedly, picks up the shoes, and then heads off in the right direction.

"I knew she'd see them," he mutters, his tone a mixture of annoyance tinged with reassurance that Mommy was on the job.

I recognize his tone of voice, and mine as well, in fact. We are copying the cadence of mother and child down through the ages. We are chanting the litany of responses chiseled in stone when the first child tracked mud into the cave. Some days are like that. My playing the role of policeman; his denying all culpability.

"Put the toys back. You know you're not supposed to haul them all out at once."

"No food upstairs. Eat that at the table; otherwise you'll spill crumbs everywhere."

"Turn off the television set; you've seen enough. Time to get dressed. It's a beautiful day outside."

"No story until after you get ready for bed. You haven't even brushed your teeth yet."

I don't enjoy hearing myself any more than my children like listening, but inevitably it happens. Mother becomes the heavy. Somebody has to keep an eye on things, and somehow she has the best vision for the job. She excels at seeing what has to be done. She becomes the guardian of good nutrition, the commander of the clean-up detail, the referee of every battle, and in charge of all the other thankless jobs that help ensure a child survives to maturity. Her tombstone shall be inscribed: How about a piece of fruit instead?

Even when I want to lighten up, automatically I find myself saying no. I can no more stop issuing orders than I can stop scratching an itch. Justifying yourself by reminding your child that you're saying these things for his own good sounds about as riveting as a speech about taking your vitamins or drinking milk with every meal.

In a way, the more you act like a Mother, the more you start to lose your place as your child's best friend. Subtly, the relationship shifts. Mommy used to tickle your toes; now she reminds you to put on your shoes. She's the pacifist who buys you nothing when the only new shoes in your size carry a picture of G.I. Joe. Kids are no fools. If Daddy will let them sneak an ice cream bar, watch cartoons, or make a mess, they will prevail upon him to let them do it. And they will conspire to make Mommy feel she's being unreasonable and ill tempered to protest.

As a child, I remember wishing my mother would relax and loosen up a bit. I remember the living room that under her authority was declared off limits. I remember the terror in my heart when I accidently broke a vase, and the dinners I endlessly pushed around on my plate because I was forced to finish them. (I ate dinner the way my husband folds laundry: I spread everything out in piles, hoping it would look like I was making progress.) It was always my father who messed up the kitchen after dinner by making us popcorn. But I never once remember his making us pick up our rooms—or even his cleaning up the kitchen, come to think of it.

Now I see my mother's point of view so clearly, it's frightening. Sometimes I hear her words, and they are coming out of my mouth. And sometimes when I see myself in the mirror,

I look just like her. And sometimes, when my son casts a long-suffering look in my direction, I fear the transformation is complete. I have become my mother.

ACTING your age is one thing, but feeling it is quite another.

Sometime after the birth of your baby, you will cuddle his darling face close to yours and gaze lovingly into the mirror.

But watch out. The contrast between his fresh face and your seasoned alternative may be more than you can handle. His unlined skin is a rebuke to you—you and your mouth that has launched a thousand smiles. A baby's skin is petal soft; you buy creams and moisturizers that make you smell like a garden but never quite leave you feeling like a flower. His elbows are dimpled and smooth; yours look like they've been braking bikes across asphalt. I find it hard to believe my muscles ever could have started out so firm. Certainly if my thighs had been as great as my daughter's, I would never have let them deteriorate to their present condition.

Children deserve credit for sending parents into tailspins of depression. They not only force parents to act their age but also to come to terms with it. Their very newness offers a silent rebuke to a parent's gradual and previously unnoticed deterioration. They can leave you feeling old and grumpy.

It's not as if children allow you to feel good by letting you sleep or rest. For at least a year they leave you colored by a grainy layer of fatigue. I'd look fresh also if I took a nap whenever I wanted. As kids get older, the seesaw upends even farther. Almost in vampire fashion, children seem to thrive while they drain adult efforts and energies. As the hyperactive toddler draws upon an unlimited energy source, your battery seems to wear down. Late in the afternoon I have watched my son wantonly ride his big wheels in relentless circles, giving kamikaze yells, while I shuffle into the kitchen to debate internally whether peanut butter sandwiches can be considered a nutritionally adequate dinner. Had anybody warned me that my children's youth would red flag my own aging, I might have recommended childbirth for someone younger.

Children make you feel your age. One mother says she used to attend her high school basketball games after graduation and still feel like one of the students. That fantasy became impossible, she admits, once she began balancing her daughter on her hip. Perhaps what slammed it home for me was swinging at the playground. As a child I used to love it: pumping my legs up toward the sky, twisting the chain tight to let it unwind and spin me around. My children also love to swing. Yet now, even when I swing sedately with a child in my lap, the motion makes me sick to my stomach.

With the same unfairness, children get to eat as much as they want—something else I used to like to do. An infant probably consumes countless times his body weight in fluids per day, and we relentless parents urge him to eat more. We try to talk toddlers out of cookies and candy, but only rarely is it because they are overweight. They practically eat nonstop, but you'd never know it. Four year olds actually wear belts because something has to hold up their pants. Yet while children suffer no ill effects from putting on the feedbag, Mommy is fighting waistline creep and reading articles about how it's easier to put on the pounds as she gets older.

Part of the problem, I comfort myself by saying, is not that I am so old. It's that preschoolers are so young. It's the new version of the old generation gap. Preschool children are at an age where losing a baby tooth is a status symbol. Chronologically, I am closer to wearing dentures. I am dealing with an age where the big thing is to undress all of the dollies. I'm old enough where I feel uncomfortable around anyone naked. My children are ready for lunch at the time I used to rouse myself for breakfast. I am, in short, too old to be watching Pound Puppy movies and pretending that I like them.

Not too long ago when a woman taking a telephone survey asked if anyone in my household wore diapers, I thought it was funny. When she asked the family income, I was only mildly put out. But when she asked my age and then assigned it to the oldest category, I was downright upset. The feeling was similar to the time a visitor pointed to my wedding picture on the mantle and asked me who was in it.

When my college class held its fifteenth reunion, the officers sent out a survey about our attitudes and accomplishments. I stumbled over this question: What has been your biggest accomplishment over the last five years? The answer is easy: Producing three children. Dealing with the implications of that answer is not.

When it comes to being a parent, maybe younger mothers cope better. Their bodies bounce back faster from pregnancy and labor. They are less likely to throw out their backs picking up toys or 30-pound children. They may be less likely to know better. They have fewer carefree days to remember before baby-sitters and sibling rivalry—the days before the bathroom became a potty. Younger mothers wouldn't feel out of step answering my questionnaire. They produced their three children ten years ago and are starting their careers now. Now they may be coping with adolescence, but they also are able to take as long an uninterrupted shower as they want in the mornings. Sounds like an even trade to me.

Children are our links with immortality, but they also remind us of our own mortality. Their birthdays remind us that ours are passing. Children may be the sunshine of our lives, but they also denote an eclipse. If they act like children, we cannot. It's almost unfair, this unintentional way children torture their parents. It also explains, of course, why the grandparents are smiling.

4   How the Mighty Have Fallen

FOR the first time in quite a while, my husband and I recently entertained people neither related to our children, nor parents themselves. This means they were not particularly interested in seeing my son display his foot-deep pile of artwork picture by picture, or in listening to my daughter belt out "Twinkle, Twinkle Little Star" more than two or three times. They talked about just-released movies I won't see until I can rent them. They talked about new restaurants when I haven't gone to the old, and about television shows on past my bedtime.

Trying to focus my conversation in their direction at times felt like trying to steer a grocery cart with a sticky wheel. My thoughts wouldn't go in the direction I knew I had to head. As a parent, I have gotten out of practice.

Now I'm not saying I've gone round the bend. I don't go out to dinner and then try to cut up the meat for everyone at the table. I don't remind strangers to potty before getting in the car, and I know almost as much about Barbara and George as I do about Bert and Ernie. But in the years A.C. (after children), I find my interests and my lifestyle have changed considerably from what they were B.C. (before children).

Only children could compel previously normal individuals

to discuss bowel movements at the dinner table, to haul out the photo album at the slightest provocation, and to proudly display crayon scribbles on walls previously graced only by expensive prints. I compare antibiotics with other mothers. I shop at discount stores where I never previously had set foot so that my children will have clothes to wear while playing in the dirt. I have nearly run the car off the road reaching for a cassette of *The Three Little Pigs* because a hysterical child is tired of *The Wizard of Oz*.

Once you acquire them, children become as fascinating as interest rates and points—two subjects only remotely of concern until you finance your house. Then you discuss the prime rate at the breakfast table and eagerly compare notes with other buyers. You can bore the heck out of friends who rent. Children can inspire the same obsession. Before pregnancy you say this self-absorption won't happen to you, but of course it does. You say you will keep all your childless friends, but of course you don't. You say you'll go to concerts and movies just as often as before, but of course you can't. Children change you.

It's a seductive process, and even your best friends hesitate to tell you how hard and how fast you have fallen. Your husband can't do it; he's the one you go out to dinner with and then sit talking about the children. I remember one night when we were tired but forced ourselves to attend a social obligation. At the restaurant beforehand, my husband suggested perhaps we should just eat, skip the reception, and go home. I rallied, realizing one of us should keep our priorities in order. "We can't go home yet," I told him. "We have to stay out at least until the kids are in bed."

Friendships feel the impact of children first. When one woman is going to have a baby, and the other has not, the conversation can become so one-sided it tilts. Valiantly, childless friends try not to let their eyes glaze over as you chat endlessly about layette lists, fetal monitoring, the merits of spanking, and the advantages of a sling versus a papoose. A baby shower is designed to help welcome an impending new arrival, but sometimes it can usher out an old friendship.

Friends from your childless days act as if you are no longer the same. Many of them with no children act as though you are embarking upon a journey to a destination where they have no wish to travel. You no longer can stay awake as late as they do; they fail to understand why you have to feed the baby the precise minute they choose to telephone. Party invitations can start to dwindle in the face of your regrets, but you are high on the list when anyone plans a baby shower—and then your seniority makes you the life of the party. Women who never cared before suddenly want the details of your labor and delivery.

I can remember the awed respect I accorded a colleague whose pregnancy was six months ahead of mine. It was like I had been driving behind her. Suddenly, the road took a big dip and she dropped from sight. When she resurfaced, she was showing off her new baby while I was caught in traffic and still waddling with mine. More important, she had crossed the great divide and actually survived what I could only anticipate.

Now I find myself adopting a sage-like attitude toward expectant mothers: smiling slyly as they vigorously maintain that a baby is not going to really change their lifestyle; biting my lips as they tell me how bored they would be "just staying home." I don't tell them that an infant at three months bears small resemblance to a baby at six months. I keep my I-told-you-so's to myself.

Friendships, you find out, come more naturally with other parents. Automatically you find yourself feeling closer to other mothers; you are bunkmates at the same camp, inmates at the same prison. Suddenly, you appreciate someone who can tell you that bananas bind. Children have brought me closer to other parents I previously hadn't gotten to know. When we moved into our neighborhood as a childless couple, we didn't have much more in common with our neighbors than part of an address. We did a lot of waving in passing. But now that we have children, we see our neighbors all the time.

Children can be the glue that holds many a friendship together. When your son fishes in the gutter with the boy next door and your daughter cooks mud pies with the girl two doors down, the mothers have at least a mess in common. When your kids both go to the morning session of kindergarten, the mothers probably share a noontime carpool.

Children will acquaint you with the intimate details of your neighbors' lives. You will find out when they nap, eat dinner, and go on vacation: the times, in other words, when their children cannot play. You will feel pressure to keep up with the Joneses' kids. You will notice new clothes, shoes, and haircuts, and investigate every new toy a neighbor's child has— partly because your child is begging for something identical. Likewise, many a mother has weaned her baby from the bottle or pitched the pacifier because the little boy next door already has gotten rid of his.

You will learn the mother's coming-home-at-the-end-of-the-day prayer. It goes: Please don't let any of their friends be playing outside, so I can get them all inside the house and get the doors closed without a fight. Homes that previously you had never entered you will barge into without a second thought as you chase after your disappearing child. Phone numbers will become familiar as you routinely call to inquire: "Did you know Sara has wandered over here all by herself?" The only homes on my street I have never been inside, and the only neighbors I do not know, are the ones with older children. The "wheels" in their households are cars; in my household they are bicycles.

Neighbors you get to know first might be those who live closest—about as far away as a one year old can walk. The farther your child is allowed to roam, the more parents you will know. My husband and I were foolish, we realize now, to worry about the size of our back yard. Children, who want to be out in front where their friends are, rarely agree to use it. They want to be where the action is—and they take their parents with them. Children warm up a chilly neighborhood. In fact, the only thing that can get the neighbors talking faster is finding out the sale price of the house at the end of the block.

When I have the time to think about it, I realize that in addition to my friendships, children have changed me in other ways I never would have believed possible. They have influenced not only my attitude toward pregnancy and childbirth, but they influence the things I say, the things I buy, and the places I go. I have downshifted lifestyles at a time in my life when a good baby-sitter is more valuable—and far more practical—than a diamond tennis bracelet.

I remember going shopping for our first car when we were childless. My husband asked what kind I wanted and I told him: cute. He laughed at me, but I knew exactly what I meant. I like cars that are sleek, steerable and, well, cute. The kind you can tuck neatly away inside the garage and small parking spaces. The kind that never hold more than four passengers. The last time we went shopping for a car, my husband didn't ask what I wanted. We both knew it didn't matter. As a family of five, we were shopping for a "full-sized car." We were shopping because our original car, still cute as a button, was no longer big enough to hold the entire family at once. We bought something big and un-cute.

When it comes to being consumers, we are the All-American family now. Everything we buy fairly screams children.

Recently we went shopping for bunk beds. Civilian grown-ups don't sleep in bunk beds. Who buys them? Parents expecting their second or third baby, of course. Immediately after purchasing the bunk beds, I went shopping for vinyl mattress covers—the odiferous kind that crinkle when you turn over but which also protects the mattress from leaks, spills, and other natural disasters. "Oh, good luck with the potty training," laughed the saleslady as she rang up my purchase. I hadn't even told her.

Likewise, at the grocery store the details of my life quickly can be scanned off my cash register tape. Weekly I buy apple juice and milk by the gallon jug; the diapers and jars of baby food speak for themselves. I live in the cold cereal capital of the world. The picture is completed by the economy-sized bottles of glass cleaner and the ever-present mega-container of laundry detergent. (My washing machine is the only appliance operating more than the television. I suffered postpartum depression only because it broke the day I came home from the hospital.)

Occasionally my purchases lead me to ponder how far I have strayed off the garden path. Clearly I can remember when I was younger how I hesitated to buy a new couch and retire my college-dormitory furnishings. I didn't want the responsibility of taking care of a couch—my first piece of major furniture. If I ever decided to go backpacking through Europe, first I would have to store the darn thing. I felt the same way when my husband and I bought our first house. It was an infringement on our mobility, on our ability to pack up, change jobs, and change cities when the mood struck.

With three children, of course, those issues are moot. I can't even change dinner reservations without advance planning.

Now I have the furniture (especially beds), the house, and the curbside alongside which I weekly deposit my All-American garbage. Into it goes empty cereal boxes and full diapers, party hats from birthdays gone by, orphaned puzzle pieces, and empty juice bottles.

But if the inventory of my life is taken by my purchases, it also is revealed by what I do not buy. I do not buy the pale wool carpeting, the off-white couch, and the new furniture I would like. I do not buy the crystal vases and glass knicknacks that catch my eye. And my silk and linen blouses hang in the back of my closet. They are out of style and won't be replaced. Like the dangling earrings I no longer wear, they make too tempting a target. They all belong to the era when I didn't wear a bathrobe over my dress until I have kissed everyone good-by. Now my car keys double as a teething ring, and my lifestyle is anything but sleek, steerable, or cute. My life, in short, drives like a station wagon.

As a consequence, I now crave what I cannot have. Because I am surrounded by chaos, I now crave order. I remember longingly the days when my household was quiet and dinners were punctuated only by orderly conversation. Now I yearn for the chance to go anywhere alone without having to explain to somebody why I am going and what I hope to accomplish.

All of which explains the appeal of grocery stores. The stores in my neighborhood now remain open 24 hours a day. This never meant much to me personally before—but that was before the weekly shopping became my form of therapy. For years I would take the two kids with me to shop. We could, I told myself, enjoy quality time. I taught them facts such as the color of carrots. As a sort of public service, I was careful to go mid-week when the stores wouldn't be as crowded with impatient shoppers. But since having three kids, I have taken to shopping alone. Totally. Whenever my husband can watch the children. Grocery shopping is practically the only time I leave the house alone; the only time I can put my purse in the car seat instead of on the floor, the only time I can walk past the toy vending machines without an argument.

I admit it. For years I used to smirk at women who shopped at night, but now I understand. The grocery store has a symmetry my life has not. Nothing in my house ever can be found in the same place twice. At the store the food is organized on the same shelves on the same aisles every week. When I shop alone I organize my coupons, lovingly placing all the cereal coupons in one place and the diaper coupons in another. I actually take a moment to think about what we might eat the coming week—and I never have to assume guard duty outside the washroom, or bolt from the checkout line to drag my son away from the candy rack. Long check-out lines don't faze me. In fact, I rather enjoy the chance to stand still.

Something about three children inspires in me a craving for neatness, order, and predictability—those things I no longer have. I long to go out for lunch without dodging nap times or worrying whether a toddler's patience will be gone before the food arrives. When I work at the office, my desk is so neat it appears uninhabited. "This is the only territory over which I have control," I tell amazed coworkers. "My life at home increasingly resembles a war of attrition against the barbarian hordes of chaos. My desk is the only place I have to myself."

With children in the house, objects are subject to gravitational pulls unexplained by the laws of physics. To get to the washing machine in my garage, for example, daily I must climb over one big wheel bike, one bike with training wheels, one tricycle, a fire engine, and one plastic car. They appear to be locked in orbit. I'd put up a "No Parking" sign, but nobody can read.

Recently all of us went to dinner at the apartment of a single friend, and I was knocked over by a strong wave of nostalgia. I remember those days when my perfume bottles sat prettily on top of my dresser, and little feet didn't totter around in my good shoes and then leave them under a bed. Those were the days when the pillows were always in place on the couch—because nobody had used them to build a fort. My friend had her necklaces hanging from pegs, and without even measuring I knew that one two year old plus one stepstool easily could add up to total destruction. My friend had her stereo equipment sitting out low in the open—more fascinating to little fingers than a busy box could ever be. We filled my friend's apartment to overflowing.

Our visit reminded me of the story about the people who complained their house was too small. Take in a cat, they were advised. They did, and the house became even more crowded. Get a dog, they were told. They did, and it got worse. Then they were told to bring a horse inside. Life became impossible. They had no room at all. Finally, they were told: Get rid of the animals. They did—and suddenly their house that once had seemed cramped now felt enormous. Well, I feel the same way about my children. It's tempting to reflect how the house would seem bigger without them. But I keep reminding myself it also would seem empty.

IF children have changed my life in ways I never expected, they also have changed the way that I've expected. A pregnant mother is not the same as an expectant mother. I was excited and uncomplaining when bearing my first child, but I was impatient and demanding when bearing my third. During my last pregnancy I knew what I was getting into—and in the hospital I knew what I was trying to get out of.

It wasn't until my third pregnancy that finally I admitted, the bloom was off this rose. Just as I had lost the knack for cocktail conversation, so I had lost the knack for gracefully gaining 30 pounds. My spirits were wilting and my self-image (unlike the rest of me) was starved. I remember debating each morning whether to hike my slip up over my enlarging belly or hitch it under. I remember wearing unbuttoned, straining blouses beneath jumpers and telling myself it didn't matter what I looked like underneath. I can remember how my friends started to study my stomach, gauging its growth, before making eye contact with me. So I talked with my hands a lot to remind them that I still had great wrists. I did not have great ankles. I mourned when I realized my ankle bones had put in their last public appearance until after delivery. I remember trying to find my hip bone so I would have something upon which to balance my other children.

I told myself I was not the only patient in the world whose cruel doctor insisted on weighing her each visit; or the only mother who would lie to her children by saying she had no idea what happened to the rest of the graham crackers. I was not the only mother whose coworkers organized a lottery as to when her rapidly expanding belly was going to burst. And I definitely was not the only mother not in potty training who never strayed far from a bathroom. I just felt like it.

Maybe love is lovelier the second time around, but the song never mentions a triple play. Pregnancy and childbirth are wondrous experiences, the first two times. I had sailed through them energetic and proud. But the third time, I did not feel lovely at all. Part of me just kept wondering: How did it ever come to this?

If I had expected to have three children, I probably would have invested in a dress-for-success maternity wardrobe. But since each time has been "the last time," I've been a borrower—not an investor. The third pregnancy, my children began to ask me why I was always wearing Daddy's clothes. In my seventh month, my mother dragged me shopping, claiming it was food for my self-esteem. I went only after I calculated that if I bought a new dress and wore it once a week for the next two months, it probably would get as much use as a normal dress gets in a year. Turns out virtually everyone noticed and was grateful to see me wearing something new.

The maternity shops were filled with women all about three months pregnant. They were using cutesy pillows attached to satin ribbons to simulate advanced pregnancy as they tried on clothes. I didn't need the pillow. The salesladies shot me dirty looks as I lumbered in—proceeded by my sticky-fingered daughter and my belly that protruded proudly like the bow of a battleship. Because I was bigger than the pillows, and probably made the clothes look bad, presumably I was a poor advertisement for business.

I remember that final stage during which there was no mistaking whether I was going to have a baby. Long gone was the twilight stage when friends sneak surreptitious looks to calculate whether I was merely putting on weight. Rather, stewardesses, salesladies, and my boss gave me anxious glances as they calculated whether I was likely to do anything messy on the premises. When I washed my clothes, I realized all my shirts were spotted where my belly had bumped into the kitchen counters. But while I was wearing them, of course, I couldn't even see that part of my shirt. Likewise, I lost sight of my toes unless I sat.

But I was beginning to catch sight of the end. The doctor wanted his fee paid up-front and his nurses wanted the insurance forms completed. (Too late I discovered my insurance specifically excluded coverage for conditions self-inflicted during periods of insanity.) Even my husband finally began asking questions: "Where will we put the baby clothes? Where will we put the baby?"

But the third time I discovered I had a very wait-and-see attitude, probably because two kids already kept me so busy. That meant I decided to wait to worry about anything that didn't require immediate anxiety—and then I would wait to see how bad it was going to get. Like my weight. At the beginning I watched it. But in the eighth month, what's an extra pound when you're already dealing in double figures? "I'll get tough and lose it after the baby comes," I told a coworker standing behind me at the holiday buffet. He merely gave me a that's-what-they-all-say smile and watched me load my plate. But I knew. Once you're already over the hill, the only thing left to do is pick up speed until you hit bottom.

That happened in the hospital. The day after delivery the doctors began trying to hustle me out, but I dug in my heels. My first hospital stay, when my room had been blanketed by flowers, I was anxious to go home. The third time, my room had only one bouquet. But it wasn't wilted yet—so it couldn't be time to leave. I told my doctor I preferred to check in for at least a week. I deserved it. As a mother whose only other regular physical exercise includes bench pressing a toddler and running the treadmill of laundry and grocery shopping, having a baby is the maternal equivalent of going for the gold. Every muscle was sore. Equally important, I had a pretty good idea what was waiting for me at home. I knew three kids under the age of five would outnumber one mother.

Hospitals, on the other hand, have a lot to recommend them. For the first time since my husband and I went on vacation two children ago, I could order what I wanted to eat. Then somebody served it to me in bed and on time, and I got to eat it while it was still hot. When I didn't feel like moving, the bed would do it for me. A nurse would even draw me a bath, something I previously could picture only in my imagination. I understand when a grown-up takes a bath it has something to do with being alone in a room and relaxing.

True, hospitals now have these unlimited visitation policies, but I simply imposed limits of my own. My husband would bring the two older children for a visit, and then take them home when I got tired. I could have the new baby in the room, available for their inspection, or ring for the nursery to come take him away. Personally, I preferred to install him in the nursery when his siblings were around. That way, they could view him through a thick wall of plastic. I toyed with the notion of installing such a wall at home as a way of insuring he would survive to celebrate his first birthday.

I have to admit, however, that hospitals will never quite replace the Golden Door. As health spas for the misbegotten, they have their shortcomings. The third time, I was critical enough to spot them. My hospital did not have labor-delivery-recovery rooms in one. Instead, I was shunted from room to room. The minute a nurse got two gurneys within 50 feet of each other, she would smile across the chasm at me and say, "Now scoot over, Mrs. Zarnow." She might just as well have said jump. And the latest in cozily decorated maternity rooms doesn't count for much so long as the nurses insist on waking you up to ask how you're feeling. Then they don't believe you, anyway. In the dead of the night they wheel up some machine that sounds like a fork lift to take your blood pressure and verify that you're feeling all right. I wouldn't want a nurse's job, of course. I couldn't imagine constantly asking exhausted women to turn over, looking at something unmentionable, and then pronouncing it beautiful. I sit on it and I know otherwise.

But given all those drawbacks, I wanted to stay in my half of a hospital room a little longer. I felt like the bride who spent months planning the wedding, but never considered married life after the honeymoon. When it was time to leave the hospital, suddenly I could foresee my future. I knew I would spend my days chasing after two children while my hands were already full carrying a third. I knew I would be discussing teething more than the news, because thanks to the former I would rarely be able to stay awake long enough to watch the latter. I knew there would be more dirty diapers in my garbage and less opportunities for me to sit down during dinner. In other words, I knew my three children were going to be with me the rest of my life. And unless you count the grocery store, that hospital was probably my last chance at a semi-private room.

5 I Never Thought I Would . . .

WHEN my son at nine months developed fear of water, I let him take his bath with me. When we potty trained our son at three, we left bathroom doors open so he could see what we were talking about. When my mother came for a visit, she was horrified.

"You can't let a little boy see you get into the shower," she admonished me. "Where is your modesty?"

Well, I may have had some once, but no longer. I can pinpoint the exact day when I lost it. Sometime during the 12 hours it took to deliver my first baby. It started with an enema and ended with a command performance before an audience of five or six doctors and nurses, complete with mirrored walls and flashing cameras.

Giving birth is hell on a sense of modesty; rearing children is even worse on your inhibitions.

The photos in my family album that record childbirth are all perfectly discreet. But I don't care what "birthing alternative" you choose—the experience itself is in no way discreet. I remember graphically telling my husband where to go while I was in transition. He had been foolish enough to tell me how my contractions ought to feel. Depending upon your personal tolerance of pain, what you say or how you look during labor probably becomes the last thing on your mind. That's fortunate, because during labor and delivery your "private parts" fail to remain that any more.

Later, if you nurse your baby, you will become accustomed to relinquishing absolute privacy over certain other portions of your body. Many a woman who starts out retiring discreetly to the bedroom, often ends up matter-of-factly feeding her child in the living room. Otherwise you'd never get to be in the living room. No matter where you sit, you often will find yourself delivering an illustrated anatomy lecture for curious older children.

I remember one time at a family party when I needed to nurse my baby. I waited until all the guests went outdoors, and then sat alone in the den to feed him. One of the husbands walked back in and offered to keep me company. His face was a study in struggle when belatedly he realized what I was doing. His urge to be embarrassed fought it out with his desire to remain blase and cool. We sat and talked, his eyes focused on a spot just above my forehead.

Since having a baby, I rarely am allowed in the bathroom alone. Even when I batten down all the doors, undeterred my daughter will invite herself in and pull back the shower curtain to check and see whether Mommy is finished yet. The toddler pushes on the door to get inside, and at least once a day it fails to latch and he succeeds. If I really cared, I would install a lock on that door.

Ironically, while a mother's feelings of modesty and privacy are being battered into nonexistence, she finds herself in the position of teaching her children to have them.

Young children prefer to run about naked and barefoot, and there is nothing nasty or evil about it when they do. They want to explore all their moving parts and talk about it afterward. You learn to talk matter of factly with them as you identify and catalog everything. So where is a child's modesty? I don't believe they are born with any. And to teach them modesty, I'm not quite prepared to teach them shame. This does not mean, however, I have not delivered lectures about self-respect and private parts—conveniently defined as anything covered by a bathing suit. (So far we have placed only parents and doctors on the approved list for touching.) Sometimes, instinctively, you know when going *au naturel* has gone far enough. As one mother put it, "The time comes when other adults on the beach are offended at the sight of your child without a bathing suit." My son wanted to know how babies come out. When I told him, he asked me if he could watch. I never hesitated before saying no.

BUT while giving birth to my children damaged my modesty, living with them is destroying my inhibitions. My modesty eventually will recover; my inhibitions may not. Like decrepit buildings, my children are tearing them down for good. Having spent my entire life in a headlong rush to grow up, my children are teaching me to grow down.

For purposes of imagination, we have converted the grocery cart into a train. My daughter, seated up front, bellows at the top of her lungs: "All aboard!" My son, standing by the back of the basket, screams: "Choo-choo!" As we head around the corner, even I chime in: "Chug, chug." We are noisy. Since we also are the only train in the produce department, we attract a lot of attention—most of it good-natured smiles. Everyone understands. I am not the only mother who has learned to behave like a kid.

I remember every Tuesday how I used to run in circles around the room and flap my wings. Yes, that's right. My wings. My daughter would wave a scarf in her hand (the sort the women driving convertibles used to wear on Route 66) as she would grin mightily and pretend to soar like an eagle. I stumbled along beside her, trying to feel graceful and wondering why I didn't feel as foolish as I undoubtedly looked. Next we were baby birds, hatching from our shells. The two year olds spread their scarves on the floor and scrunged up into their shells. Here is where I finally would draw the line. And as I glanced around the room, I noticed none of the other mothers at the mommy-and-me music class were down there, either.

There are, after all, limits. But education and professional experience did not prepare me to know what they are. Since becoming a mother I have danced a creditable version of the Hokey Pokey in public. When it comes to enjoying your children, ordinary standards no longer apply. Children take adults back to pleasures we used to pretend we were too sophisticated to enjoy. They give us an excuse to enjoy them.

That is why I found myself, enjoying myself, one night at the library during pajama storytime.

Twenty heads swivel upward, mouths slightly open, as the boys and girls lose themselves in the story. The boy wearing Smurf slippers sits cross-legged next to the girl clutching a teddy bear, both engrossed as they hear about the little girl afraid of the dark in her brand new bed. She takes so many stuffed animals to sleep with her, she falls out.

"I only take two teddy bears to bed with me," my son stands up to offer in the way of sage advice. Nobody smiles but the parents in the audience. Stories, after all, are serious business.

As the librarian begins another book, some of the younger children begin to lose interest. Really too young to sit still, they are there because their parents liked the idea of their being there. For parents, the library brings back memories. Children love books about Harry the Dirty Dog, Katy the kangaroo with no pockets, or Curious George the monkey—books parents remember because we loved them. The children's room, with its pint-sized tables and chairs and low shelves, is part of childhood. It represents a time when a good book had more pictures than text, and reading it meant getting to sit on somebody's lap. It was a time when homework wasn't yet a vocabulary word, and life was perpetual recess.

Together with my children I recently watched *Peter Pan* for the first time in years. I had loved it as a child. With every birthday cake, I remember closing my eyes and earnestly wishing that I could fly. I remember how I cried when Peter came back for Wendy—only to find she was all grown up.

I felt a bit like Wendy introducing Peter to her daughter, when it was time to introduce my children to the show. I told them they could stay up late because a wonderful program was going to be on television. They knew about Peter Pan from books, but they had never seen the movie. I didn't know what my children—who were bored by *Bambi*—were going to think. Flying is a pretty tame special effect for a generation that takes *Star Wars* for granted. Children, as Peter put it, know such an awful lot these days. Finally came the moment of truth. Peter Pan, whose intelligence was nothing to crow about, decided to drink his poisoned medicine despite Tinkerbell's warning. So she drank it instead. Her light dimmed, and Peter implored the audience for help. If you believe in fairies, he said, clap.

My son clapped.

"Clap louder," said Peter. "Louder."

We all clapped, as loud and as hard as we could. My children clapped because they believed in the story, and I clapped because I believe in childhood.

The next night, as I tucked my daughter into bed, she asked: "Mommy, are there really fairies?"

"Well, some people say they are real and some people say they are not," I said. "Nobody knows for sure, so you can believe in them if you want to. Do you believe in fairies?"

"Yes," she said. "No. I mean, well, do you believe in fairies?"

"Yes," I said. "I believe that certain moments can be absolutely magic."

"Good," she said, snuggling under her covers. "That's what I wanted to think, too."

Children carry you back to other things. As a parent you find yourself taking neighborhood walks after dinner and bike rides to the park. You rediscover pinwheels that spin in the wind, soap bubbles that pop just out of reach, and the feel of wet grass beneath your toes as you run through the sprinkler. Relentlessly you play "Row, Row, Row Your Boat" with a child who neither knows nor cares that the game is not battery-operated or advertised on television. Don't be surprised at the revival of a primordial urge to plant a garden, grow a sweet potato in a jar on the window sill, organize family reunions, or decorate the house for holidays. You scout out museums, puppet shows, and patriotic parades with fervor. Childhood today does not resemble a Norman Rockwell painting, but you want to sketch in some of those images for your child.

Little events become big and important in a small world. A new dog on the street draws a crowd, and we dash across the yard to view a visiting butterfly. We are excited when the neighborhood park is blessed with new slides and rings. It is an honest-to-gosh event worthy of discussion at the dinner table.

Children give parents an excuse. One time, in a moment of insanity, I agreed to let my daughter, then two, push her plastic shopping cart down the grocery store aisles next to mine. It sounded like a good idea in theory, but in practice she becomes a minnow swimming upstream against the current of other shoppers. Nobody sees her; worse, she does not look up to see anybody. Even the grandmothers who might have smiled indulgently at the family scene seem less than charmed as they are forced to maneuver their carts around hers in the middle of every aisle. I carry it off with aplomb, although I won't do it again. My daughter is only young once, I reason. Adults go shopping every week.

A few weeks later we are at the library for story hour. The librarian, who already has made her fashion statement by wearing a hat made out of newspaper, is organizing the children into a hat-wearing marching band.

"Let's have a few of the moms join in," she says—no doubt striving for legitimacy as much as for company. She offers the wooden-salad-spoon instrument to the mother standing next to me. After that mother shrinks self-consciously against the wall, I find myself once again keeping time to the music. Beneath the baby's spit-up stains on my sweatshirt must be a sign that reads: "Soft touch. Ask her." So I parade around, make noise, and smile. Either I am enticing the children into enjoying themselves, or they have tricked me into behaving like an idiot. Does it matter which?

What's the point in being embarrassed among children? The only time my son successfully has embarrassed me is once in a restaurant. I had lowered the baby under the table, covered his head with my shirt, and crouched over him to supply an emergency transfusion of milk. The five year old inquired at the top of his lungs: "Mom, why are you showing your private parts in public?"

Recently, a friend called and asked if it was a bad time for me to talk. "No, it's fine," I reassured her. "I just put a diaper on the baby and he managed to pee on my pants."

"Oh," she offered. "I'll hold on while you change your clothes."

"That's all right," I answered without hesitation. "I wasn't going to."

 ❧

YOUR children will carry you to new highs: moments of noble sacrifice and selfless love. They also will drag you down to new lows of desperation and levels of behavior you never previously would have believed possible.

It is 4 P.M. near the end of a long day with Daddy out of town, and my major concern is how soon I can put the children down to bed and put my feet up to rest.

"Time for baths," I gaily announce an hour early, hustling everyone into the bathroom. "Time for dinner," I announce at 5:00, under the correct assumption children can eat at any hour. "Ready for bed?" I query at 6:00—a full two hours before normal. "All right," I concede as I pull the bedroom windowshades down against the glaring sunlight, "I guess you can stay up a bit longer." I ask again at 6:30. By 7:00, convinced they have gotten away with forbidden extra time, the kids admit they really are tired. By 7:30, all are asleep and all's well. And of my deception I am not the least bit ashamed.

We parents play tricks upon our kids. Without batting an eyelash, I have thrown handfuls of my children's Halloween candy in the garbage while their backs were turned. To dissuade my son from a flashy box of Ghostbusters cereal in the grocery store, I shamelessly have told him to buy Product 19 because the number means only big kids can eat it. For nearly two years I successfully had my son convinced yogurt was what other people referred to as ice cream. Other times, I have taken a 30-minute drive on the way home from a just-down-the-street errand in order to lull a cranky toddler to sleep. I have taken presents given my daughter when she was too young, hidden them in the closet, and six months later re-wrapped and given them to her again. I told my son that liquid soap is called "germbusters," and I told my daughter that if she sucked her thumb she would end up with "witches' teeth."

Parenting is a humbling experience. This is so particularly if you aspire to improve upon your own parents' performance and instead find yourself doing no better.

I saw my mother in me one morning when we all had gone out to breakfast. If he had not been my child, I would have left my son at the restaurant table along with the dirty dishes. He was whining, crying, sniveling, and utterly spoiling my meal. He whined because his pancakes were slow in coming. He cried because Daddy cut the pieces too big, and then he sniffled because Daddy cut them at all. He could not sit up and he could not be quiet. He responded to neither patient under-standing ("We could glue the pieces back together with syrup . . .") or threats ("If you don't stop, I'm taking you to the car for a spanking . . .").

Suddenly, unbidden, words welled up in my throat along with my anger—words I never fully had understood before.

"If you don't stop," I snarled, "I'll give you something to cry about." They are, I realized, the words my mother used to hurl at me.

Parenting is humbling for a second reason. It forces me to admit the depths of my own pettiness and the degree to which I am willing to compromise my previously held high standards. I am, for example, at times willing to let my children do almost anything in exchange for some peace and quiet.

"Snails have slime juice," the boy next door solemnly in-forms my son.

"Yes," he replies, as they survey their captive. "Let's squish some out."

Lazily, in the outfield of my attention, I watch them brandish sticks like scalpels and prepare for surgery. "Squish some over here," says one boy. "Squish some out from the shell," says the other. "Look how slimy."

Vaguely I monitor the activity of my son, Marquis de Sade in sweats. He is inflicting a child's mindless form of torture on one of God's creatures. But I—a mother who won't even let my children stomp on a library book—don't intervene. They are, after all, keeping busy.

When it comes to co-existing with your children, I've discovered the secret lies in trade-offs. You trade them the chance to do something messy or gross you previously never thought you would allow (translation: something neat and fun). In exchange they give you a little time off.

Let them enjoy themselves making a mess upstairs piling every stuffed animal in the room on top of the bed. At least you know while they are doing it you have an uninterrupted opportunity to clean up the mess downstairs. You use safety locks to keep your kids out of every kitchen cabinet except for one, filled with plastic that you are willing to sacrifice. At least you know you can cook dinner.

A trade-off is the reason I have had this conversation:

"Did I wake you?" a friend asks over the telephone. "Your voice sounds funny."

"No," I reply. "I'm just bending down picking Play Dough off the floor.

My friend pauses. "Oh," she says, striving for a neutral tone. "You let them do that inside the house?"

You betcha. I have let my daughter peel the labels off every crayon in her color box, and it was worth a blissful half hour— even counting the time to pick up the peels. On the second consecutive rainy day I might even let her peel my vegetable cans. I have let my son cover himself in wet sand from head to toe because it translated into two hours of intense activity.

And I have let both children "cook" every petal off the daisies in my garden.

Once a few years ago, badly in need of a nap, I discovered the lengths to which desperation can drive me. My standard attempt at nap synchronization had failed. The two year old managed to awaken before I had successfully gotten the baby to sleep. Lack of sleep makes you brave. I sat the two year old and four year old down in front of their favorite movie. I offered them all sorts of dire predictions about what would happen if they strayed into trouble while I slept, and visions of the paradise and ice cream bribes that would ensue if they behaved. Then, despite the possibilities for disaster, I slept.

I had entered into the trade-off as a consenting adult. It could have been worse. When I awoke, the two year old was bouncing maniacally on the couch. With each bounce, like a confetti-throwing wedding guest, she scattered pieces of tissue from the box her brother had helped her reach. And as I later sat on the floor, refolding the mound of tissues back into the box, I decided once again the trade-off was worth it. The tissues cost less than a dollar. The nap made me feel like a million bucks.

As a mother, I do other things I never would have expected before. When I was pregnant, I never thought I would tell a pregnant woman horror stories about labor. In the same way, before having babies I could not imagine myself lying in bed listening to an infant scream in the next room, waiting for the racket to wake up my husband. Before I had toddlers, I never imagined I would starve them for three hours before dinner in the hopes they might eat some fish—or that I would put the french fries in the middle of the table as a bribe for eating all their meat. Of course, neither would I have imagined serving hot dogs or macaroni and cheese for dinner, because sometimes it's easier to swallow my pride than to argue with children who will swallow nothing else.

My children, I used to believe, never would watch cartoons on television, play with pretend guns, eat cookies in the grocery store, or taste candy. Once upon a time I also used to think they never would eat in the car. In my mind, my kids were always clean, dressed in adorable outfits, never had snotty noses, and did not pick their nails. As I said, I used to have those standards and I used to hold those expectations. Now I have children—and pretty soon it will be my turn to teach them about the tooth fairy.

6 Roles Are Nothing to Play At

BECAUSE he refuses to relinquish the TV control box, I wrench it from his hand.

"You can't do that!" shouts my five year old son.

"Yes, I can," I answer in a don't-mess-with-me tone of voice. "We are done watching television now. The show is over and we are not going to switch channels."

"Well, don't grab things out of my hands," growls my son as he flounces off in a huff. "It's my body and I can do whatever I want with it."

We have, I realize, come a long way. He was my firstborn, after all, and I spent hours examining, exploring, and adoring every inch of his baby body. I worried over every move that he made and how he learned to make it. But just as he once sent me scurrying to the library to read about child development, my son now drives me to read about discipline. As the oldest, he is the child from whom I expect the most and sometimes get the least. I applaud his every achievement; his every accomplishment to me is always a first. But as my first I feel his failures most keenly. He is often the first to feel my fury, the first to see through me, and the first I see trying to deceive me.

My son is the family trail blazer. Every stage of his is new;

every problem uncharted. I make my mistakes with him; he, in turn, will teach me to be mellow for the others. The only child who was able to enjoy being an only child, he now faces a lifetime of having to share. His way will not be easy. As the oldest he was the first child to enjoy my total love, and now he will be the first to test it.

Because my oldest son demands attention as his birthright, I can understand how it could be easy to shortchange my daughter. Her role in life is that of a middle child. I recall one Monday morning at work recounting to a friend the latest antics of my five year old and the latest virus infecting my one year old.

"That's right," said an acquaintance, leaning over to join in. "You have two children now, don't you?"

"No," I answered, "I have three."

"Really? I thought you had two boys."

"No," I responded. "I also have a daughter, in the middle."

"Oh," he said. "You never talk about her."

I ponder that comment and wonder whether my three year old gets short shrift because she's less quotable than a five year old or because she comes in the middle. My daughter is sandwiched between a big brother who always does everything first, and a baby who as the youngest does everything last. She cannot decide whether she wants to stay up late like the big boy or curl up in somebody's lap like the little boy. At three she thinks she knows everything about the world of which she knows nothing. I hear her count the crackers she receives for snack: "One, one, and one more."

According to theory, the middle child is ignored but self-reliant, the pivotal child when everyone gangs up two against one. In my family she is, of course, also different because she is a girl. But while my daughter is feminine, she is no hothouse flower or clinging vine. The theories neglect to mention that the middle child can be as assertive and hardy as a weed. I compare her to the against-all-odds dandelion that manages to flourish in the crack in the sidewalk. Surrounded on both sides by cement, with limited room to spread, she sinks her roots and flowers. She is difficult to ignore.

She knows her own mind. "Go potty," I tell her, "and then let's get you dressed."

"No," she replies with no respect for logic. "I need to get dressed first." Then, after she is dressed, she summons immense dignity, marches to the bathroom, and takes off her clothes to go potty. (In this respect, she is ahead of her big brother. I know when he has to go potty before he does.)

She is smart. When she climbs into my bed in the morning, she is careful to elbow me out of the way so she can lie where I already have warmed the sheets. She is learning to unbutton her shirt. I am a rapt audience as she undoes one button, stops, smiles at me, and says: "Wait, don't clap yet."

Very little deters her. "I need help," she announces as I pick her up from preschool. "I'm having trouble with Michelle; she makes me angry."

"I'm sorry to hear that," I reply. "How does she make you angry?"

"Oh, she won't share her Popsicle necklace with me."

"Well, it's nice to share. But sometimes you can't make somebody share. What do you want Mommy to do?"

My daughter smiles sweetly and replies: "Kill her."

And finally, my daughter, this middle child, is determined to get her share. My husband sits at the table to examine his hand.

"Ouch!" he announces. "I don't believe it. I've got a glass splinter in there."

My daughter begins to cry. Clearly her heart is about to break. I ask: "What's the matter with you?"

"I want one, too," she demands. "I want a glass slipper."

Clearly my daughter is her own person, but frequently I see her as a unit together with her big brother. They form a contrast to their younger brother. He is considered the baby; they are not.

I remember taking all three on an expedition to the grocery store, and more than a few fellow shoppers appraised us with quizzical glances. No wonder. The children were wearing summer sandals on their feet and winter hats on their heads. In between, my daughter, two, wore a summer party dress and sweater; my son, four, wore his pants inside out.

Unless your children have begun picking out their clothes or dressing themselves, you would have no inkling how this attire came about. As a mother whose son was learning to put his own clothes on and whose daughter was learning to take everything off, it seemed perfectly normal. When she managed to untie her shoes, I bit my lips not to remind her that I had just put them on. When he struggled for ten minutes to pull on his shirt, I wasn't going to be the one to tell him it was backward. (Hell hath no fury like a four year old whose arms are tangled in his shirt sleeves). Usually, by the time I had one fully dressed, the other was again naked.

It's enough to make you appreciate babies. A four month old does not quibble when you truss him up in blue velveteen coveralls with a picture of a goose ambling across his chest. A four year old refuses to believe he ever wore anything so ridiculous. The antidote to the preschooler's declaration of independence is the newborn. Tired of a smart mouth that sasses more than it smiles? Have a baby. A newborn cries, but it's hard to take his screams personally. Tired of addressing your child's back as he walks away while you're talking to him? Have a baby. For a few months, at least, you know an infant can be found right where you left him. Tired of arguing over snacks and meals with a child who would order a hamburger at the Four Seasons or inspect a fly on the floor of the Cistine Chapel? Have a baby. They eat the same thing every day and never complain about the monotony.

Compared to toddlers, a baby is a soft touch. He only wants to be fed, changed, and held . . . constantly. A baby merely wants you to satisfy all his bodily requirements the instant he realizes what they are. Babies, with simple needs and simple wants, are less complicated than older siblings. But as a mother of three, I have yet to decide which age I prefer. I cannot decide whether I would rather be aggravated or simply exhausted.

My toddler, of course, is no longer a baby. But after turning his sister into a middle child, for the rest of his life he will remain this family's youngest—the baby of the family. I review his status now because he needs a haircut.

The hair in the front of his head, all 15 months long of it, grazes his ears and falls into his eyes. The hair on the back of his head, however, is what claims my attention. It twists into ringlets, hugs the shape of his head, and uncovers the sweetness of his neck.

I know that his hair needs to be cut. Strangers are starting to confuse my "he" with a "she." To my mind, of course, there is no such confusion. To me he is every inch a boy—from the way he charges at my knees with a kamikaze cry, to the way he goes mountain climbing on the furniture. But although I know inevitably the time is coming; somehow, I hesitate to cut those curls.

My son will, of course, be just as adorable with his hair trimmed. His legs still will pudge out and he still will have a 100-watt smile. He still will allow me to dress him in shirts decorated with dancing elephants and to make him wear a jacket because I feel cold. But he will look older. The minute his hair hugs his head and lays flat all around, my baby will be gone.

Previously, I always had mentally wrinkled my nose with disdain to hear mothers mourn the growth of their babies. What else, after all, are children supposed to do? So what if they leap-frogged from an 18-month size into a Toddler 2? So what if they walked at nine months? I have never approved when I see a three year old riding lump-like in a stroller with a pacifier and bottle. But suddenly I can understand how the youngest in the family always remains the baby in the family. This is probably my last rug rat. I'm in no rush to think of him as growing up.

I am from a family of four children, and it wasn't until the youngest turned 30 that I realized we were growing up. If the "baby" was getting older, after all, then so was I.

As a mother, I see no reason to hustle ahead my youngest. As he charges off to inspect the world, he sucks his thumb and drags along his blanket. I try to restrict the blanket to when he is tired or hungry, but that's as tough as I'm going to get right now. When he is bigger and able to pluck it himself from inside his crib, then I can foresee a problem. That blanket could become a tattered fixture. When he is too old to be sucking his thumb, then I can foresee that habit becoming a problem. But right now, I cannot bring myself to worry. He is just too plain cute. As the baby in the family, he's entitled to act that way. Age is his excuse.

When his older brother and sister are watching television, he loves to change the channel. It frustrates them, and they post themselves on guard duty to protect the TV dial from enemy attack. We tell the baby to stop. We tell him he is making us angry, but it's not easy to make the point to a one year old. When his older brother and sister are listening to books, the baby is too little to listen as well. He tries to grab the book I am reading. Sometimes he will tug his sister off my lap and away from the place he perceives as exclusively his. My children groan, and together we move to either include him or to outsmart him. We tell him to stop, but it's not easy to persuade a baby.

We excuse him now on the basis of immaturity. It will be several more months before we can hold him to higher standards of behavior. The danger is that because he is the last child, we might continue to excuse him after there is no excuse. We will have to remember that while he will always be the youngest in the family, he will not indefinitely be a baby. A cutie today can be a brat tomorrow.

For now, however, he remains too adorable to take these matters seriously. He still waddles when he walks and he looks positively cherubic adorned by his curls. He needs a haircut, it's true. But for at least a while longer, my baby is not going to get it.

I USED to think that haircuts not only turned babies into children; they turned them into boys or girls. When I had only a boy, my theory was that many toddlers have no inkling of their sexual identity until they get their first haircuts. If the cut is short, they realize they're a boy. Girls get bangs. Now I also have a daughter and I realize that's not so. Toddlers still in bibs have latched onto Mommy or Daddy as role models. They exhibit copy-cat characteristics. As a toddler my daughter would place anything with a purse-like strap over the crook of her arm and wave bye-bye. Now, as a three year old, she selects a plastic purse when I offer to buy her a present. My son likes to take his shirt off and go out in the backyard to do some "work." When given free run in a toy store, he chose an imitation power drill.

I know a girl who is the third child in a family of boys. Suffice it to say she lives in a household of Cub Scout meetings, camping trips, and karate.

"I take her to the games," says her father, "and talk with her about how great a sport softball is and how she could play as well as any boy if she wanted to. I build it up really big. Then, one day, I asked her if she wanted to practice with me and see if she could make the team someday. She twirled around and told me she wasn't interested—unless she could be a cheerleader."

Today parents don't rear their daughters to be teachers, nurses, or secretaries. You can be the principal, the doctor, or the boss, we tell them. We give our daughters toy trucks and let our sons play with dolls. Deliberately, we tell our kids to ride their abilities as far as they can take them—determined that outmoded sexual stereotypes will not apply the brakes to a child's potential. Like many modern parents, my husband and I try not to rear our daughter differently from our sons. He can learn to cook and she can learn to throw a mean curve ball. Yet somehow, although we teach them the same things, they learn differently. I want to rear a son who will become a different sort of husband than his Daddy—one who doesn't mind cooking or doing the laundry. It sounds egalitarian, but it doesn't always work.

Some of their preferences seem totally innate. My daughter immediately loved stuffed animals; my son had no interest. We gave her a doll. She calls it her baby, feeds it, and forces the poor thing to nap constantly. I confess to whispering in my own house because she has demanded that I be quiet; her baby is sleeping. At a comparable age, we gave him a doll— which he proceeded to decapitate. He likes meat and potatoes;

she prefers salads. Boys experience a magnetic attraction to sticks, stones, and squishy bugs. Their pockets are bursting by the end of each walk; I have put rocks through the washing machine. A boy is likely to wipe his nose on the carpet.

Girls tend to be prissy by comparison. Of course they get dirty, but they also immediately want to wipe their hands of anything sticky—and they can get downright distressed if something spills on their clothes. My daughter used to make me change her bib if it got too messy. Little girls can be as irresistibly drawn to frilly dresses as little boys are drawn to sticks. For nearly two years I was able to dress my daughter in the clothes that covered my son. Coveralls and t-shirts suited her just fine—until she was old enough to notice what the other girls were wearing. Now she wants to wear a dress to play in the sandbox. She's already into fashion; she requests clothes for her birthday. Her sense of style tends toward glitter, bows, and twirling skirts. If I wear something new, she notices before my husband.

She lusts after a lipstick to call her own. "Mommy, you're so beautiful," she says adoringly. "You're more beautiful than I am."

"No," I modestly demure. "We are both beautiful in different ways."

"Mommy," she insists. "You're more beautiful because you get to use makeup."

My neighbor's daughter regularly runs around in ballet costume. Once I naively asked where she takes lessons. "Oh, she doesn't take lessons," came the reply. "She just likes the costume." Then I remembered how I, who can trip over a paperclip, once took ballet lessons because I wanted to wear a tutu.

But as a mother I rebel against permitting my daughter to

believe changing clothes is an athletic event. I do not want her to paint skin that already looks the way cosmetics promise to make it. I want to bolster my daughter's self-esteem by praising what she does as well as the way she looks.

It won't be easy. Consider my daughter's hair. The parents of girls spend a considerable amount of time talking about hair.

"You have beautiful hair," we say nightly as we unsnarl our daughter's locks after bath. This is both an effort to make her feel good about herself and to encourage her to sit still during the inevitably painful procedure.

But I suspect flattery has gone too far. The other night after my husband finished baths, I overheard my daughter say: "Let's talk some more about my beautiful, long hair."

One day I tried to teach her that being beautiful is not the highest accolade. I told her the story of the ugly sister who was as sweet and good on the inside as she was unappealing on the outside. She did not, in other words, have long hair. But this girl was so beautiful in her heart, I told my daughter, that she even forgave the unkind girls who teased her. I waxed quite eloquent on that score.

"So you see, it's nice to be beautiful on the outside," I concluded, "but it's more important to be beautiful in your heart."

"Oh, I have a beautiful heart," my daughter informed me. "I do good things for other people."

She gave a little skip as we walked along.

"But I'm also lucky," she added. "I have beautiful long hair."

In addition to their early concern with appearances, they say girls mature faster than boys. I see the truth in that; skills come to them sooner. They are faster to walk and faster to talk. Their emotions are less straightforward and more complex. If a little boy gets angry, a little girl gets angry and then gets even. My son gets in trouble for hitting; my daughter doesn't hit, but she knows how to defy. Already I can see who will be the handful as a teen-ager.

Likewise, nobody takes charge like a little girl. One day the children are outside making piles in the sawdust from a home improvement project, drawing pictures with discarded planks. It's good, clean, freewheeling fun—until the five-year-old girl in the neighborhood comes along. Within seconds she has everybody organized: "You go here, and you go there. Now, let's push our piles together in the middle."

By the age of five, boys and girls begin to recognize their differences and they stop being best friends. Usually the girls pull away first by making the boys feel totally inadequate. Little boys are no match for the self-assurance of little girls. My son used to play often with the girl down the street until she took up with other girls. Now when they do try to play together, it often doesn't work. They play differently. She starts doing cartwheels he cannot copy and then baffles him by fetching some plastic horses and announcing, "Let's play ponies." My daughter and her girlfriend play "dollie wollie" together or pretend to be kitty cats. My son and his buddies turn sticks into guns and play at war.

I recall one particular day when my son tried to play with this five-year-old friend. They were pretending to be trains. Furiously they pedaled their bicycles to the corner and then speeded back, yelling "red light" as they screeched to a stop. This is my five-year-old son's kind of game. The level of noise was exceeded only by the speed of his legs. He was in heaven; his friend was not.

"Let's play Barbies," she announced brightly. She dashed inside her house to return with her Barbie doll and a stuffed dog. "I'm playing with the Barbie," she said, dispensing the dog to my son.

Then she proceeded to sit atop the erstwhile traintrack and play with her doll. This involved spending a great deal of time flipping Barbie's long blonde pony tail and maneuvering her legs into the splits. "Barbie is dancing," she informed us. My son threw the stuffed dog on the ground in disgust and stalked away.

The five year old, abandoned, sat a few minutes alone on the sidewalk. That takes care of that, I thought to myself. I wondered whether she had been put in her place, or whether she even knew it. Later that same afternoon, I found out the answer.

Once again the sidewalk society had assembled outside, indulging in the latest neighborhood fad of playing with umbrellas. My son and his buddy were running around making crazed animal noises and swinging their umbrellas. Eventually they set up their umbrellas in a corner of the lawn. They had made a fort.

The girls had constructed their own structure. The five year old's lavender umbrella leaned cozily against her girlfriend's striped one as they perched on a blanket and pretended to have tea. They had made a house. The two boys came charging over, prepared to remodel the premises. The five-year-old girl looked up, straightened up, and regally intoned: "This is the living room and you boys can't come in."

COMPARED to girls, boys have ants in their pants. My son would rather be up a tree than sitting down quietly anywhere. If his sister runs, he charges. If she sings, he sounds like a barnyard. He gyrates ceaselessly.

"Can't you be quiet and sit still?" I asked him once, in exasperation.

"Mom," he replied with surprising candor. "I can't even stand still."

Little boys strike me as a mixture of John Wayne and Don Quixote. In snapshots my son usually appears wearing t-shirts stretched out of shape and shorts displaying bruised and battered legs with dirty, knobby knees. The photos do not show the dialogue behind those bruises. I remember the first day of shorts weather the spring when my son was four and his shin was about to lose its virginity.

He catches his toe on a crack in the pavement, falls with all the grace of a wounded elephant, and skins his leg. The cut measures less than an eighth of an inch, microscopically deep— but it does draw blood. Two drops. My son saw them.

"Mom, this is a terrible owie," he whimpers as he limps beside me toward the car.

"We'll put medicine on it when we get home," I say.

"But Mom," the four year old stresses, "this is the worst owie I have ever had."

"No," I say. "The worst was when you took a nose dive from the top stair of the slide in the playground when you were two. That was a magnificent mess."

"I don't remember that," he says as we drive home. "This one is terrible." He blubbers. "I want to call Daddy."

Inwardly I marvel: Was this once the infant who used to crawl off the grass in order to drag his bare knees across the sidewalk? Back then he never flinched. At home, a regular Clara Barton, I cleanse the wound and apply a bandage largely for dramatic effect. "All done," I announce in the chipper sort of voice the dentist uses after drilling for 45 minutes. "Aren't we better?"

No, we're not. We call Daddy at the office for sympathy. We make lunch for sustenance.

"I want to see the doctor," he announces, too distraught to eat.

"No," I say. "That's not necessary."

"Yes, it is."

"Well, how about we call the nurse and you can tell her about it?" I compromise. "Remember, both the doctor and the nurse can help you."

"That's right," he replies, "but I need to see the doctor." My son tries to be conciliatory. "I need your medicine *and* the doctor's medicine," he says.

"Trust me," I sigh. "I've treated hundreds of owies in my lifetime and yours does not require further medical attention." Eventually, my diagnosis wins out. We give the wound and its scab some further attention, but two days later it is totally forgotten. Two weeks later into shorts season and the only thing more scarred than my furniture are his legs.

I venture into the backyard one afternoon, made suspicious by the sudden silence. There, I find my son has scaled a chain link fence, pole vaulted across a chasm, and is dangling from the roof of the playhouse.

"Get down from there!" I shriek. "What are you doing up there? Do you want to kill yourself?"

"Mo-m-m-m-m," he answers with unflappable calm, "I'm all right. It's just that I need to climb." Big boys, he assures me, never get hurt.

And that, I understand, is the way it is with boys. After first blood, they think they're Rambo.

7 The Earth Is Flat: The World According to Children

MY daughter, starving for her lunch, tears apart the sandwich I have just put together.

She doesn't just eat it; literally, she tears it up. First she takes off the bread, then she removes the pieces of turkey, swings them between her fingers, and lowers them into her mouth. The center of the sandwich devoured, next she concentrates upon the bread.

I view her performance as somehow typical of the relationship between adult and child. We look at the same thing but each sees it differently. I see the sandwich as something to make by putting it together; she sees the sandwich as something to eat by taking it apart.

Children, to recycle an old expression, have minds of their own. They have always had them, but parents usually don't notice until after the first year—which is when children start to do what they want and not necessarily what they are told. Somehow, it's like eating the sandwich: Grown-ups and children look at the same task and approach it differently. They understand the world differently.

A child's understanding of events relates only to what he previously has experienced. Nothing is real until it has happened to him.

A friend's father used to spin long accounts of his war days, stories to which she would listen avidly as a young child. After such a session, she recalls asking her father: "Daddy, were you killed in the war?"

I remember telling my son about the big family reunion we were going to host. "Let me tell you what that means," I said. "All kinds of aunts, uncles, grandmas, and cousins will be coming to visit. It will be very exciting. Like a great big party."

"Oh," he answered. "What kind of cake will we have?"

A child has no notion of time. He remembers events and conversations with no regard to context or how long ago they happened. My daughter has informed me that, yes, she remembers when Mommy was a baby.

A child's sense of justice is swift and merciless. Do not be appalled when your two year old spies a bug on the ground outside and shouts: "Kill it! Kill it!"

Adults concentrate on the table-tops of life, but even on tip-toe our kids barely can see over the edge. To deal successfully with children, we need to remember the shorter point of view. How often, after all, do you clean the top of the refrigerator?

My husband has lost his car keys. They might have remained missing but unmissed amidst the chaos flourishing inside his den, but he needs them this minute to start the car.

Logically I ask: "When did you last have them?"

"The baby was playing with them this afternoon," he replies a tad testily.

"Then look for them in places a baby would put them," I respond with maddening calm. (They aren't my keys, after all.) "Look low."

Surveying the floor from the vantage point of his hands and knees proves successful. The keys are wedged under the desk chair.

When I was pregnant, my son wanted to know if I had

to get married again because I was having another baby. A perfectly logical question to a child, and not necessarily a bad idea.

Too often adults forget to view the world from a child's perspective. On a visit to the library I found a perfect example. I was camped out in the children's section, selecting books I would read to the kids that week.

"I have to potty," my son desperately announced.

"You know where it is," I replied, a bit distracted. "Just remember to wash your hands." A few minutes later he returned.

"Mom," he said, "the paint won't wash off."

He had my full attention. I paid a visit to the bathroom. There, on the front of the bathroom door, were two, well defined, pint-sized sets of handprints—right below the sign he couldn't read. It said: "Wet Paint."

To the extent that it's a matter of perspective, I think it comes down to ours versus theirs.

Children reason differently. Their sense of logic is computer-like and literal. Expect your two year old to notice that his clothes no longer fit—and expect him to ask you why they keep shrinking. In a variation on the chocolate-cow question, my five year old wondered if hot water comes from the hot part of the ocean. Likewise, I can remember a visit to the barber that led to a big discussion about how hair grows and why it needs to be cut. My son kept insisting hair couldn't grow because we never water it.

Another time some men were trimming the trees around our house. "Look at the mess those guys have made," exclaimed our four-year-old neighbor. "They knocked branches down everywhere. What a mess. They're gonna have to pay you a lot."

A child sees things with a narrow focus, with none of the

ambiguities that clutter adult perceptions. This can make conversations tricky.

"What did you have for lunch?" I ask a three-year-old neighbor.

"We had french fries for lunch," she says.

The Nancy Nutritionist in me cannot leave it alone. I ask: "Is that all you had?"

"No," she answers. "We also had ketchup."

Another example. After you hear the thud and the cry, have you ever tried to find out from your child what happened?

You ask: "Where did you get hurt?"

She points: "Over there."

You say: "No, I mean what did you hit?"

She says: "The floor by the stairs."

Finally, you say: "Show me your owie."

She looks at you as if to say: Why didn't you just say so?

My son has the same kind of literal, tunnel vision. His teacher is talking about tigers and how they are endangered by man. "There used to be lots and lots of tigers in the jungles," she says. "Now there are millions of people in cities and only about 8,000 tigers." My son raises his hand with a suggestion: "How about we kill the extra people so there are only about 8,000 people, too?" My son wasn't so much concerned with the means as he was with the equitable end. He saw a literal solution to the problem. He didn't think about who would be killed, so much as getting them out of the way.

When my daughter was three, we had a long discussion about how far down the block she could ride her bicycle alone. Despite her protests, I insisted she go no further than Emily's house.

"Oh, Mom, that's not far enough," she responded unhappily, clearly wishing Emily would move. "Oh, why does Emily have to live there?"

On the first warm day of spring, when my son was four, he pointed to his shorts in the drawer and asked: "Can I wear my short-sleeved pants?" Likewise, after getting undressed, he has asked me to outside-in his shirt.

My neighbor relates this story about her four year old's response to the "Farmer in the Dell" (Daddy planted a seed) explanation of conception:

His first question was: "Didn't it hurt?"

"No," she responded, swallowing a smile. "I wouldn't say it hurt at all."

"But Mom," he continued, still a bit perplexed, "I understand that Daddy planted the seed. But then how did he get the dirt in?"

No wonder children, little more than newborns when it comes to their reasoning ability, are gullible targets. Recent surveys have found that despite explanations otherwise, the majority of second and third graders still believe the earth is flat. When my daughter was two she had a toy can that sounded "meow" whenever she turned it over. I asked her: "Is there a cat inside?" "Yes," she responded with complete assurance, "but a very small one."

One time, when my son was four, I remember leading him on. Sauntering over to the counter, he had picked up his new gumball toy and then casually strolled to a position behind my back. I heard the pop of the mechanism being opened and then the sound of a mouth chomping on forbidden fruit.

"You're not supposed to be eating those now," I said conversationally without turning around.

"Eating what?" answered the voice of innocence.

"You know," I said. "The gumball."

"Well," he asked, "how do you know?"

"Because I have eyes on the back of my head," I earnestly informed him.

"You do not. I've never seen them."

"Well, that's because they're covered by my hair," I responded. "All girls grow them when they become mommies. How else did I know what you were doing?"

Skidding between his disbelief and the slick surface of my seeming logic, my son let the matter drop. I didn't know how convincing I'd been until a few days later when he ambushed me from behind and combed through my hair trying to find the extra eyes. I confessed and apologized for teasing him.

Sometimes, I have to wonder if he is teasing me. One night, aware that I was being a bit of a grump, I tried to explain myself to my son.

"Daddy is away on business," I said. "I'm trying to make you understand I need you to be a helper. There are three of you kids and only one of me. I shouldn't have to ask you three times to put your dirty clothes in the laundry. You know they go there. I don't like to ask you any more than you like to hear me."

"If you dump your clothes on the floor," I continued, "should I just leave them there? If we all dumped our clothes on the floor, we'd just end up with a giant mess. Somebody has got to make sure we pick up, and it always seems to be me. Don't you understand it's hard for Mommy, especially with Daddy gone? There's so much to do and I've only got two hands."

My five year old paused at this explanation, gazed shrewdly at me for a moment, and then sagely nodded his head.

"I understand, Mom," he said. "Don't you wish you were an octopus? I think it would be easier for you if you had eight hands."

Ultimately, from any perspective, a child's main priority is himself. (This also may be true for adults but we are more sophisticated at covering it up.) So when it comes to viewing the world, a child's concept of geography is skewed: He sees himself as the center of the universe.

My husband shows our son on the map places where he used to live. "Here's where I grew up; here's where I went to school; here's where Mommy and Daddy used to live before we moved here."

"I see," responds my son, not seeing at all. "Mommy," he shouts, "come and see where Daddy used to live before he came to live with us."

PARENTS must understand what a child considers important: his own happiness. A child's own wants come first in his priorities. Understanding these priorities does not necessarily mean an adult can share them. Children choose their cereal by the prize on the box, they choose their restaurant by the prize inside the kid's meal, and they rate a school on the basis of its playground equipment. My daughter selects her clothes based on the picture on them, and my son picks his for their pockets. They both rate toys by their commercials.

Living with those standards can be hard on a parent. My husband's modest ambition in life at this point is to watch the evening news without interruption and with some comprehension. That remains, however, an ambition.

The anchorman discusses a troop reduction proposal; open hostilities break out between the five year old and the three year old. A Cabinet member gives his views concerning the economy. They remain unknown; the three year old has dumped the entire box of Legos.

"Be quiet," my husband thunders. "Daddy wants to know what is going on in the world." The children, quite obviously, do not. They do, however, want to hear the commercials. Our son gives avid attention to a commercial touting the virtues of a family sedan. Our daughter memorizes a catchy jingle singing the praises of a watch.

It's all a matter of priorities—theirs versus ours. My children find the commercials important, not the news. Any day now I expect them to ask us to be quiet during the commercials. Children are not unreasonable, obstinate creatures. They simply see the toys on the floor as proof of what a good time they had playing. We see only the mess.

But where there's a will, there's a way. And if you can bring your child's priority into agreement with your own, he will be willing—and able.

The five year old seemingly is incapable of getting dressed. Legs stumble on their way into trousers; socks hover over toes for minutes without coming in for a landing. But tell that same child he has two seconds to get dressed because his best friend is waiting outside, and miraculously, he will manage. Ask any mother whose child is dressed before dawn on the morning he goes to a birthday party. She will tell you that if he wants to do it, he can do it. The same logic applies to eating. You may see the peas as an end unto themselves. The child may eat them only if he sees them as a means to dessert.

The other night, well past bedtime, both children suddenly settled down to quietly look at books. The sudden silence was as deafening as it was luxurious. So delightful was the quiet that my husband and I allowed them to stay up a good half hour extra just to enjoy it. I'm still not sure whether their priority was to read the books or to stay up late. In either case, they were successful in rearranging our priorities.

Bathtime also is misunderstood. Parents see it as an opportunity to ascertain that every part of a child's body starts out clean at the same time; children see it as a chance to play. Thus, we think they should get out of the water after they are washed; children do not agree since the fun is just beginning.

Consider potty training. When my daughter was nearly three, I considered it a priority; my daughter did not.

She knew exactly what she was doing—or in this case not doing. She didn't want to take the time and trouble to use the potty. Her space-age disposable diapers kept her too comfortable; she saw them as a convenience, not as the shameful badge of a baby. I saw them as keeping her out of preschool.

"Big girls use the potty," I would tell her, trying to rearrange her priorities. "Big girls wear beautiful panties," I would try to entice her. "Big girls get to go to big girl school." (Remember, when you are little, big is beautiful.)

"I don't want to be potty trained," she informed me. "I don't want to go to school."

"But when Mommy goes to work, you would have to stay home with a baby-sitter," I cajoled her. "You don't want to do that."

"Well," she drawled, glancing at me shrewdly. "Are you going to work right this minute?"

ネ

I AM washing off the chicken in a dinnertime performance before an intent audience of one.

"Once upon a time," my son asks, "did that chicken used to be alive?"

"Yes," I answer, mentally holding my breath and waiting for the first accusations from a newly-awakened vegetarian conscience.

"Oh," answers the little Darwin I apparently am rearing. Then there is silence.

The moment passed, but I have not forgotten. Every parent knows such moments of bated breath. I call it the Uh-Oh Pause. It's that freeze-frame moment when you are poised at the pinnacle of the roller coaster, knowing that from there on, it's all downhill. You know the descent will be rapid, and you know the landing will be hard. It is the moment after lightning strikes and before the storm of anger or revelation follows. Frequently, it is the moment before you know you are in trouble.

It can be the instant when you see the baby toss his pacifier just out of reach as you are driving down the freeway. Before he starts to scream, you experience the Uh-Oh Pause. It comes when you see your child's just-purchased helium-filled balloon drift upward in the early stages of interplanetary exploration. It's when your son is watering the grass with the hose, and he turns toward you to answer a question. But often it comes just after he asks you a question.

Children ask a lot of questions. Like a blizzard, a child's questions come down fast and furious.

Where does a worm put his feet?

What do butterflies eat?

Why do farmers have haystacks?

Why do daddies have whiskers?

What shape are our teeth?

Even inquiring people may not want to know, but chances are your youngster will. Suddenly, the data base of knowledge with which you have skidded by for daily existence is insufficient. Your child, who doesn't know enough to be embarrassed by a question, will ask. He will ask questions, countless questions—pinioning you with his curiosity and dissecting your credentials as an infallible source. You will scramble to remember tidbits from every science show you ever watched.

Children worry about things adults never even begin to

consider: "Mommy, if a Martian came down from space and he landed here and he decided to shoot us, would it be on the news that night?" Their concerns and the timing of them are different. As I am in a hurry, struggling to parallel park, my daughter asks: "Mommy, does God know where we live?"

Even reading a book together is not a straightforward operation. The plot can become irrelevant as each page brings new questions. Reading *The Wizard of Oz*, we spent 20 minutes discussing the health of the Wicked Witch of the East—and in the picture she clearly is dead.

"Why is the witch dead, Mommy? Why are her toes curled? What happened to her shoes?"

Hard to imagine, but the child you yearned to hear speak, you someday may yearn to have silent. My five year old maintains such a steady stream of chatter in the car that I have gotten out at our destination, closed my door, and walked around to open his—only to find him still talking without interruption.

When it comes to answering questions, sometimes I wonder why I bother. As I launch into an explanation of what it looks like on the inside of our ears, my daughter interrupts to ask: "Did you pack something good inside my lunchbox?"

With many questions, in fact, I'm convinced that at least half the time it doesn't matter what words a child is saying. If you listen closely, she's really only asking the same question: "Mommy, won't you listen to me?"

So when it comes to answering questions, I always try. I can offer only one absolute rule for parents on the rack: Never lie in the face of inquisition. If you don't know, say so. Simplify if you will; try not to distort. This has taught me not only to give honest answers, but the reverse: to ask only honest questions. I don't ask unless I'm prepared to hear the answer.

I have watched a woman, eight months pregnant and bursting with life, ask her toddler: "Wouldn't you like to have a new baby brother or sister?" She pats the swollen stomach her child has not yet noticed.

"Not really," comes the succinct reply.

At dinnertime, when my son's hands are so filthy it is difficult to discern where the nails begin, I myself have asked: "Wouldn't you like to wash up?"

"No," he answers even more succinctly.

In the face of such answers from children, and sometimes after a long day of grilling that leaves your patience more threadbare than the elbows on your favorite shirt, I say go ahead. Answer your child the way he often answers you: Because. You have my blessing to do this. Personally, I am more likely to do this with questions that begin "why." They are infinitely more difficult than those that begin "what." Perhaps this is because you can't just answer them with a fact; you have to grapple with a reason. On the other hand, you don't necessarily have to answer all questions, either. A non-answer, satisfying in its logic, may suffice.

Question: "Mommy, why is the sky so high?"

Answer: "Well, we wouldn't want to hit our heads on it, would we?"

The danger, of course, lies in over- or under-answering a question. A child asking what a dog eats may be perfectly satisfied with "dog food," but it becomes a bit of a cop-out to say people eat "people food." Some children will get comfort from the ritual of always hearing certain responses to certain questions ("Mommy, why did you have me?"). But otherwise, as a child gets older, you don't have to give him all the answers. Sometimes, help him figure them out with you.

"Why do we wear shoes, Mommy?"

"Well, why do you think: Do we wear them in the bath or outside? What would happen if we didn't wear them?"

As your child matures, so does your answer. "Why is it nighttime?" the two year old asks. "Because the sun is going to sleep," answers Mommy, pajamas in hand. The three year old, however, is entitled to a bit more of a scientific response. Just how scientific?

Sometimes, all the knowledge in the world is useless following a question and the subsequent Uh-Oh Pause. Not even science can prepare you with an adequate response.

When our son wanted to know where babies come from, we believed at three and one half he was old enough to hear an abridged version of the truth.

"Babies grow from a seed in Mommy's tummy."

"Where does the seed come from?"

"From Daddy."

"How does Daddy plant it inside Mommy?"

The Pause follows.

Then, we tell him.

He giggles. Hysterically.

"No," he laughs. "That's not true. That's too silly. That can't be right. Tell me how he really does it."

FOR a long time, I never believed my children were capable of dishonesty.

Young children don't realize they are lying, another mother explained to me. They confuse what happened with what they wish had happened. Ask them if they saw grandma today and they will say yes, even if it was two days ago. In their minds what happened yesterday really happened today—because that's how they want it. For a long time I bought that explanation. But no longer. Children will maintain their own innocence in the face of overwhelming evidence to the contrary.

Even they must suspect they are bending reality. The miracles started when my daughter was two. She scaled the Himalaya-high railings of her crib, climbed out, threw her just-laundered pajamas on the floor, and then climbed back in. I know this happened because my son, then four, told me that was how the pajamas I asked him to put on the bureau had ended up on the floor.

A similar rash of miracles began to bless us.

My husband's car keys disappeared one morning, and he assumed a child had been playing with them. A frenzied search of the garbage failed to turn them up among the banana peels, and both kids denied all culpability. Later, after searching the house, I focused suspicious eyes on my son and delivered a mini-sermon comparing car keys in importance to his new bike. Daddy needed them to get where he was going.

While my back was turned, the miracle occurred. My son "found" the car keys in the middle of the floor. We talked gently about it for several minutes before he admitted he had found them in his pocket. He'd put them there in the morning, but had "forgotten."

I have witnessed other mysterious occurrences. The day of my daughter's second birthday, I placed her chocolate-iced cake up high on the counter so she could see but not touch it. When I came back into the kitchen later, the side of the cake bore the clear indentation from somebody's finger taking a swipe of the icing. "I didn't do it," my son asserted before I even asked. It didn't take a fingerprint expert to deduce otherwise. Eventually he told me that he did it—by "mistake."

One time I found my daughter surrounded by crayons and scribbles on the wall. She was alone in the room. I asked: "Why did you color on the wall?" Defensively she replied: "Well, did you see me do it?"

One morning I caught my son sitting at the breakfast table

eating cookies. "Those cookies were for dinner tonight," I reminded him. He stopped chewing, feigned innocence, and looked out at the morning sunshine. "Oh," he asked, "isn't this nighttime?"

My son will emerge, fists in pockets, from the bathroom where his mission has been to wash his hands. "They're clean," he says, "but I don't want to show them."

In addition to lying badly, I now believe even good children can tell bad lies. Adults have a tough time convincing children that lying is a worse crime than the original sin they are trying to cover up. And some adults don't realize the importance of imparting that message.

One day we had gone shopping at a department store. That evening, stashed behind the toilet, we discovered a pint-sized bow tie still bearing it's original $5 price tag.

"Where did this come from?" I thundered in ominous tones.

"She brought it home in her pocket," my son replied, pointing at his sister. Another miracle. The dress she was wearing had no pockets.

Then followed your standard, generic lecture on the virtue of telling the truth and the evil of taking anything from a store without paying for it. We threw in a few references to stealing, and policemen and jail for good measure.

The next day father and son paid a repeat visit to the store to apologize and hand over the goods. Unfortunately, there was not an ominous-looking, armed security guard in sight. In fact, the only saleslady in the bow tie department was a genial-looking matron more suited to playing fairy godmother than wicked witch. In solemn ceremony, my son admitted his culpability and apologized. He awaited sentencing. The saleslady beamed. "That's all right, sonny." She smiled. "Don't worry about it."

Some customer service.

My children are older now than when the age of miracles began, and I have begun to suspect my five year old finally has gotten the message that lying is worse than the original crime. In fact, a recent incident makes me wonder if maybe he hasn't learned the lesson too well. I found myself almost feeling nostalgic for the good old days when he told an honest lie.

Like the broken neck of a goose, the towel rack dangled from the back of the bathroom door. It caught my eye immediately.

"Did you see the broken towel rack?" I asked my five year old.

"No," he said. "I didn't see it."

"Well, it's hanging broken from the door and you were just in there. You didn't notice? It's a real mess."

My son glanced at me and studied the tablecloth intently. A schematic of his brain would have revealed an intense tug-of-war between the impulse to lie and the knowledge that he wouldn't get away with it. He began to speak in a low voice.

"Well, I saw it there for the first time and I decided to pull up on it," he admitted.

"You did chin-ups on the towel rack? Haven't we told you not even to tug on the towels?" I asked incredulously, unable to curb my voice as it started to escalate toward a shriek.

"Well, I just pulled on it," he offered in lame defense.

"You're too heavy for the towel rack," I explained, rather patiently I believe under the circumstances. "A towel rack is designed to hold up a towel, not a person."

His face brightened. "Gee, I must be strong."

"It has nothing to do with being strong," I said, aiming to deflate his ego. "It has to do with being heavy. You are too heavy, and you should have known better. That wasn't a smart thing to do."

Solemnly, he sat there.

"Is that all you have to say?" I asked.

"Well, I'm sorry," he pushed out, after a pause.

"I'm not sure you are," I answered. "I'm glad you told the truth, that you didn't lie. It's important to tell the truth and I know it was hard. But I expect you to know better. There won't be a next time, right?"

He nodded, the doorbell rang, and I answered it to find his buddy waiting to see if my son could play. I turned to call him, but he was gone. Upstairs, I heard him sobbing.

"What's the matter?" I asked, trying to sound understanding like the Beaver's mother.

He sobbed uncontrollably for several minutes.

"I broke the towel rack," he cried.

"We talked about that. It wasn't smart but you won't do it again," I said. "So what's the matter now?"

"Well, I broke it," he said, still crying.

"Yes, and you learned your lesson," I said. "You aren't going to do that again."

I moved in for some compassionate hugs, as his tears subsided. The tables had turned and now I felt compelled to make him feel better. It crossed my mind that somehow my son had transformed himself from guilty party into innocent victim.

"You told me the truth about it," I repeated. "That wasn't easy to do, and I'm proud of you for that."

He dried his eyes and we went back downstairs to play. Concerned that I had comforted him too much, I added a final half-serious admonition: "Remember, you do that again and I'll kill ya."

He stopped, turned, and stared at me with wide eyes.

"You mean you would put a knife through my heart?"

"No, I wouldn't put a knife through your heart," I said. "We've come too far to waste all that effort. I mean I would get very angry."

"Oh," he sighed. "I didn't know the other meaning to those words."

I glanced at him suspiciously, but he remained straight-faced. Then he ran off to play. I stood there, starting to suspect a con job.

A few minutes later he came sidling over to me again.

"How are you going to punish me?" he asked. "Do I have to have a spanking?"

"Well, I hadn't thought about it," I answered. "We'll see when Daddy gets home."

He fixed me with an ardent gaze.

"Well, when Daddy gets home, I want you to tell him all about the towel rack," he said. "Tell him how I broke it and tell him how I told the truth. Oh, and Mom, don't forget to tell him how hard I cried."

8
Don't Blame Your Mother; She's Already Blaming Herself

GROGGILY my mind swam up from the depths of a sound sleep to the surface of my consciousness.

The baby, standing in his crib, was crying. For a minute I was tempted to slide back under, to close my eyes, and submerge myself in the warm and inviting lagoon of sleep.

But I got up. Without even checking the clock, I knew it was 3 A.M. With Swiss precision, every night for the past month, my ten month old had awakened at this hour. Indignantly, insistently he would cry for my attention. He expected me to come and get him, and I did. To my mind, he was demanding reparations because I was gone during the day. Because I felt guilty, I paid.

The room was dark, but he knew exactly where I was. I could tell by the pause in his crying that he recognized the creak of my mattress as I got up. He sensed my presence as I crossed the room, and if I detoured past his crib to the bathroom, his cries would build to an angry crescendo.

My baby wanted to nurse. He didn't need to, of course. In the past he had slept through the night and awakened the next morning without any obvious signs of malnutrition. And I knew from experience that two nights of letting him scream would cure him of his nocturnal habit.

I fed him, however, because I needed to. For the first time, with a baby so young, I was working most of the day. I left him playing at home in the morning and didn't see him again until nearly dusk. He was well cared for and happy—and unaware that he held me in his debt. He exerted leverage he did not even understand. But because I could not always be there for him during the day, I wanted to be there for him at night.

Not even a year old, and already most traces of his infancy were gone. He was walking, although repeatedly I advised him this was way too soon. During the day he staggered and swaggered around the room, defying gravity and executing wide turns, dragging shoes out of closets and laundry out of hampers—and making it clear that he was far too mature to be down on all fours. His baby fat was melting in the heat of so much activity, and his smile no longer was toothless. He'd graduated from patty-cake to shaking his head "no" and pulling his sister's hair. He was becoming a toddler.

But in the heart of the night, at least for a while longer, he was still a baby. So I would surrender. I would lift him from his crib and we would nestle in the stuffed armchair that once belonged to his great-grandmother. He would give one sigh—as if to say, "I knew it would come to this"—and then nurse contentedly. One hand would curl tightly around my thumb, a silent restraining order against any sudden movements. He would eat, steadily and efficiently. When he finished, I would hold him. He would drape his head on my shoulder, shifting sometimes to change sides. His arms, which started out wrapped around me, gradually would fall limply to his sides. I could feel the tension ease as his body melted into mine. He was asleep—blissfully, contentedly asleep.

For a few minutes I would hold him like this, lulling myself back to a drowsy state. But most of all, in the stillness, I would enjoy him. I enjoyed his sturdy feel, and I enjoyed knowing that at least this once I could meet his total needs. But soon I would put him back into his crib. I would glance at the clock: 3:30 A.M. I would slide back into bed, and my sleep would be a little sweeter.

Although my sleep might be sweeter, I knew what I was doing was wrong. I read somewhere that the definition of a truly spoiled child has nothing to do with material possessions. A spoiled child, said the article, is one whose mother still feeds him in the middle of the night. If that is so, I plead guilty. I did not want to spoil my child, but it was hard for me to stop. Guilt makes you do strange things.

Let's talk about black thoughts that go bump in the night. Sometimes, as I lie in bed in the darkness and mentally close the books on my actions for the day, guilt comes and gets me. I add up my mistakes, factor in my inadequacies and failings, and then weigh them against reasonable expectations. Frequently I come up short. When I was working away from home all day, the shadows of guilt seemed longest. But even when I am home, they lap at my heels after I compare myself unfavorably to the perfection I think I see elsewhere. Of course other nights, when I am sensible, I simply fall asleep.

On the Richter Scale of guilt, deciding whether to work outside the home sets off a mother's biggest tremors. The answer feels so important. The decision becomes emotional, fraught with self-justification and guilt. It is not easy to say: I do not choose to work. And it is not easy to say: I do not choose to stay home. And it is not easy to realize that whatever the decision, usually it works out all right.

In this debate, I come down as definitely undecided. I'm not happy being home days on end with no baby-sitters in sight, and I'm not happy being gone days on end, either. It took much experimentation and agonizing for me to face this fact. I have stayed home full time, worked part-time at a job I disliked, and worked full time at a job I loved. I was partly unhappy doing them all. I am no good seeing my children too little, and I am no good being around them too much.

Guilt, I have finally figured out, is not the exclusive province of mothers with paying jobs. Even when I have quality time coming out my ears, I still can feel guilty. I have even ended up feeling guilty because staying home with my kids wasn't as great as I thought it would be.

One time I announced to my children: "Vacation. Daddy has to work, but I have the week off. So we are all staying home together. No work and no preschool."

"It's going to be grand," I promised rashly. "Every day an adventure."

"No," said a friend, "you should leave the kids in school and enjoy a vacation for yourself at home." And that would have been nice. More than anything I crave time alone to myself. But I felt too guilty to indulge.

I can remember the second day of our "vacation." Breakfast barely was over and already we had read four books, water-colored five pictures, and gone outside to blow soap bubbles and watch the garbage man. Not surprisingly, by lunchtime we were at the park. I pushed the swings emphatically, encouraged as much by my children's smiles as by the fact that the activity seemed to content them for more than 20 minutes. The mother at the adjacent swing, a more tepid pusher, smiled in the way of conspirators linked by a common cause.

"You seem to be enjoying this," she commented.

"Oh, yes," I replied. "It feels good to exorcise some guilt."

She might have been slightly puzzled, but most employed mothers understand. No matter how few hours we are away, guilt is a passenger in our lives. Guilt rides in the car along with the child we drop off for the day, especially when he doesn't want to leave us. Guilt presses heavy on the chest those days we pick him up and find that he is sick. Then, when the doctor wants to know if he took a good nap, guilt points a finger at us again because we weren't there to know.

I remember how my week at home went. I pulled out all the stops: story hour at the library, wading pool in the back yard, and ice cream bars in the freezer. We planted tomatoes and we went for bike rides. Well, it was good but it wasn't grand. It's hard to be the sole source of entertainment for your kids; they prefer a fast pace. There's an unspoken question: What do we do next? A baby may want to monopolize your arms by being held constantly, but preschoolers want to monopolize your creativity in finding things for them to do. They are eager for variety and activities and other children.

Even "full-time" mothers spend some of the day filling the time for kids who always want something to do. Two mothers with two year olds were talking at the park:

"You take them to this class twice a week," said one. "They do painting and play. We could car pool. Then there's gymnastics class the other day. So that really only leaves you two days . . . ."

And so I dedicated my week to being with the kids, and yet at its end I was left feeling slightly let down. They didn't enjoy it as much as I anticipated. Again I was left with a residue of guilt—but a different kind than usual. I was left feeling guilty that I didn't have non-stop fun being with the kids I normally miss so much. Maybe I should have done some things for me—instead of trying to do everything for them and expecting everything from them.

So by Thursday, when my son asked me how soon it would be before he could go back to school, I wasn't surprised. I didn't start feeling better about the whole thing until a week later when things were back to normal: I was putting on my earrings on the way down the stairs and reminding my son to take his lunchbox. That was the morning when he asked if we could please stay home.

❧

NO matter what schedule I have tried, the only constant I have discovered over the years is that I can manage to feel guilty no matter what. When it comes to guilt, I am a champion. I feel apologetic when I prune a rose bush. I keep wanting to explain that while this may hurt, it's really for your own good. I think this is because I have great respect for authority and doing things the way you are "supposed" to. For years, after all, I did not remove the under-penalty-of-law tag from pillows, did not freeze a teething ring, and never left baby unattended. Real mothers are supposed to be perfect. In my mind, when I do less than everything, guilt casts shadows everywhere.

I remember once when I resisted the impulse to fold the laundry, but offered instead to do whatever my five year old wanted.

So I asked: "Want me to read to you?" "Nope."

"Want me to color with you?" "Nope."

"Should we build something special with the blocks?" "Nope."

"Well, then, tell me what you would like to do now."

"Well, Mom," he answered, "I'd really like to watch cartoons."

It wasn't so much that I offered my child his mother and he preferred Daffy Duck. It's just that sometimes no matter what

I do, nobody smothers me with hugs and says: "Thanks, Mom. It was grand." I want to be graded and I want an A for effort. In the motherhood line of work, unfortunately, there are no report cards. The only grades are ones I give myself, and I've always been a tough teacher.

And so I suffer emotional whiplash. On issues big and small I am spun back and forth by chance comments and conflicting reports. I stayed home on leave for six months after the birth of each child, for example; I could not bear to leave my babies sooner. The first morning back to work, my son cried when I left him at his sitter's.

"He's old enough to know you're leaving," she said. "It's easier on the little guys if you leave them when they are smaller; they don't really know what's happening."

"True," I said, "but I wanted to spend as much time home as possible."

"Well, maybe that's what you wanted, but you made it harder on him," she said. Suddenly, I feel guilty for staying home with my baby.

Guilt is an overwhelming emotion, but nothing is too small for me to apply it.

Proudly, the five year old next door personally delivers her party invitation. My son's name is neatly lettered across the envelope.

"Such good handwriting," I compliment her. "Did you learn to write so well in school?"

"No," she says. "My Mommy taught me."

And then, aimed with lethal precision by an innocent, the sharp needle of guilt stabs me. I haven't been practicing letters with my son.

Days later, we are holding an informal moan-and-groan session on the streetcorner. I mention that I am going back to work and my baby refuses to take a bottle. I ask another mother: "Did you ever have trouble?"

"Oh no," she trills. "I've never given any of my children bottles. I wean them straight to a cup."

And there it is again: a booster shot of guilt administered by a subtle dose of peer pressure. It's not that I have done anything wrong; rather, it's what I haven't done. Another mother has done more. I thought I had my priorities straight. If my baby spits up on my silk blouse, first I wipe my shoulder—then his washable chin. But I am a waffler. I reverse the order in front of witnesses.

When I hear mothers talking about the things they do, my ears perk up. They talk about hand-painting flowers on their daughter's anklets and grinding their own baby food. My daughter is lucky to find two matching socks in her drawer, and I have emptied enough commercial baby food jars to satisfy the needs of a million art teachers. In fact, I take my daughter to buy new shoes and sink under the chair in embarrassment: Her foot has grown two full sizes. I want to apologize to my baby when I finally do steel myself to his tears at night. I thought he was teething only to have the doctor tell me a week later that, no, he has fluid in his ear.

So let's talk about the G-word. Before I became a mother, I would have sworn such things wouldn't matter. Even now, intellectually I tell myself there always will be other parents with more time, more energy, and more money to spend on their children. Intellectually I know this. I need to meet my children's needs, not those of the kids next door. But emotionally, I am a target waiting for the arrows of guilt. I am anxious to keep up. If I don't, I feel guilty. Suddenly I know the lyrics to the theme song: But everybody else is doing it. Peer pressure coupled with guilt is a powerful persuader. I see children who own more uniforms than the Army. They go to karate, tap dancing, gymnastics, scouts, soccer, and roller skating. My children go to the park.

For $30 a month my two children can take music lessons at their preschool. Music certainly is worthwhile, and both kids are eager. But $60 a month is a hefty expense on top of tuition, and they simply may be too young.

"Let's hold off," I say to my husband, "until they are older." "It costs a lot of money," I explain to the kids.

"But I always wished I had taken music," my husband says.

"All the kids are taking it and it's great," my children say.

We compromise: music for the four year old, not the two year old.

I'm left feeling faintly guilty and confused. Did we cave in or did we hold the line? I'm not even sure. When my son reads the newspaper advertising inserts for toys, I routinely deny him everything on the pages. And yet when I do buy him a no-reason present, I wonder if it is an unconscious bribe to pay him off with presents for what I did not pay him in sufficient attention. When the weekend slips by and we haven't done anything spectacular, I feel guilty. I tell myself a conversation at the dinner table weighs in as quality time every bit as heavily as an outing at the zoo. I tell myself that until I hear other mothers talk about their weekends. And I wonder: Why didn't I find time for a bicycle ride after supper?

I read parents' magazines. Who can resist? They promise to make you a better mother. But they are filled with 101 ways to entertain your children on a rainy day and they leave me feeling guilty. Doesn't anyone else ever just rent a movie? Holidays make me anxious. Every year at Halloween my insides fight it out between the part of me that insists it is a cop-out to buy a costume and the part that reminds me I am lousy at making them. I am up against mothers who begin in the summer to plan for the fall. And although I could never be one of those mothers, deep inside I feel things would be better for my children if I were.

There are two kinds of mothers in this world: The first can tell you the day before what she's serving for dinner tomorrow. We other mothers aren't sure exactly what will be on the table until we've checked what's inside that container at the back of the refrigerator shelf. We are not talking the magic of microwave ovens here, but basic organization. I gag at the thought of cooking six dinners ahead and freezing them on Sundays as the women's magazines advise. My husband gags if I ask him what he wants to eat for dinner tomorrow as he washes tonight's dishes. And I can't imagine drawing up a shopping list that actually includes everything I'm going to need for a week. But somehow, I always have believed that if this were the case—if I were perfectly organized—I would be a better mother.

My kids are neither neglected nor starving. They always have clean clothes to wear (all right, sometimes they wear a t-shirt twice, but only if they wore it before under a sweater), a lunchbox packed the night before, and we almost never run out of milk or diapers. But somehow, deep inside, I believe that if I had everything else under perfect control, we all would be better off.

I knew other mothers were one step ahead of me when I finally roused myself to buy winter pajamas and the shelves already were empty. I knew I was lagging behind when one mother told me she sets her breakfast table after dinner. I've found out other mothers don't spend their mornings searching for the other shoe, and some mothers don't take telephone messages in crayon. There even are, I am told, working mothers who never say "hurry up" in the same breath as they say "good morning."

I am not such a mother. And although nobody openly complains, privately I believe myself to be lacking. I used to be on top of everything; now, sometimes, I am buried.

"You have to let something slide," my mother advises, watching me pile stray toys on the bottom stair as I swoop about straightening up. "Great," I answer from beneath a pile of books, puzzle pieces, and a stuffed lamb. "What do you suggest I sacrifice? Clean clothes or showers?"

But since becoming a mother I have given up on perfection. Given the choice, I'll keep my children cleaner than my house. I'll take my house picked up rather than spotless. Unlike one neighbor, I refuse to mop the floors at night. The only time they were relatively spotless was when I knew somebody would be crawling on them. Now I merely keep them free of debris. Oh, I know those perfectly organized mothers. They are the kind who never end up cramming too much dough on the last pan of cookies they are baking.

So I have jettisoned perfection to make my load lighter, but I have trouble living with my decision. Now I not only feel guilty over the chores that do not get done, but I still feel guilty over taking the time for those that do. Which is supposed to come first: the chores or the child? One takes time away from the other. True, some chores can be shared with a child. I have waited patiently while small hands present me with every (unbreakable) dish from the dishwasher; I have added a great deal of mixing to my recipes in order to accommodate "helpers." (My neighbor's daughter also likes to help cook, but the only talent she has perfected is cracking an egg. That mother is running out of appropriate recipes.)

You're trying to pay bills, for example, clearly not a spectator sport. Your child wants you to read him a book. Which comes first? I admit to some confusion on this score. As a newer mother I was inclined to drop everything. But having read "Go

Dog, Go" sufficient times to commit it to memory, I became less inclined. Besides, my children no longer all nap. So then followed the period of alternation: 20 minutes for you, kid, and 20 minutes for me. Eventually we both were satisfied, although my powers of concentration were sorely diminished.

Lately, I've been much more hard-line. Let me get my chores over with first, and then I can become a relaxed mommy ready to play. That priority seems to soothe the more compulsive side of my nature. (Don't scoff. If you run around cleaning up when your kids are napping, then you share a similar nature. If you sit down with a good book and relax, then you do not.) But if this makes me more happily productive, it also makes me less happily guilty. No child is going to grow up remembering with fond gratitude: Bless my mom. She kept the house clean.

So I tell myself I can be disorganized for a good cause, but I don't really believe it. Good mothers run their households to perfection and also manage to lavish attention on their children.

Clearly, I am never satisfied. And while I recognize the foolishness in this, I can do nothing about it. I'm unhappy if my child cries when I leave him with a sitter; I'm a little bit hurt if he doesn't want to leave when I come to take him home. I get annoyed when my son wants new shoes because his sister got them; yet I worry that I do more for one child than for the other.

I can work myself up into a lather over something so simple as the artwork my children bring home from school. Those proliferating pieces of paper constitute a challenge to my integrity. I haven't faced such a tough decision since I had to select a color scheme for the new nursery. As the drawings pile up, so does the dilemma. What do you do with them? After you have papered the house, are parents allowed to throw the pictures away or should we be resigned to having them float about the house forever along with empty Happy Meal boxes? What happens if your child sees his work in the garbage?

Which raises the other dilemma: When it comes to artwork, is Mommy supposed to be a cheerleader or critic? When presented with two lines of color reposing in the remote corner of an otherwise blank sheet of paper, I have drawn upon theatrical talents and ingenuity for my response: "Beautiful! Lovely colors! Good, strong strokes!" What troubles me is knowing when to expect improvement. Should you worry about coloring within the lines, or encourage artistic freedom? I am, after all, content to laud frenetic scribbles, pink trees and purple blobs so long as doing so nurtures my kids' tender egos. But I don't want them to be ridiculed in kindergarten, either, because nobody ever gently informed them drawing is not always a freestyle event. If other kids laugh at my children, after all, that would only give me something else to feel guilty about.

A NEWBORN baby enters the world all of 19 or 20 inches long—but already the proud parents are concerned about how he will stack up. Pediatricians start it, reporting a baby's height and weight in percentiles compared to the mythical average. Soon, parents are comparing percentiles like SAT scores—and the kid hasn't done anything but grow. Now an 18-pound six month old may be built like a cantaloupe but, by golly, he's in the 90th percentile.

And the process carries over. Is he sitting up yet and isn't she crawling? Which preschool is the best, and haven't you gotten him potty trained? Going to register my son for school, a neighbor began to advise me which teacher to request. Then she stopped herself. "Heck. They're all good," she said. "We're only talking kindergarten here, not college applications."

But when it comes to your children, we're also talking competition. It's a sense of competition that not only makes us want the best for our children, but that makes us want them to be the best. If our children can't keep up, then we feel guilty. And to protect a child's interests, some parents have been known to get rather ferocious.

The after-school puppet show at the library was free, and if it sounded good to one mother, it sounded good to at least 150 more. We were doing this for our children, so against all better judgment we crammed into an "auditorium" more the size of a walk-in closet. We bounced squirming babies in the back of the room and pushed toddlers toward the front to sit behind a string on the floor as sweat pooled down our backs.

"Listen quietly," we urged silently, as the puppeteer softly began his performance for which nobody had furnished sound equipment. "Sit still," we hissed across the room, as our charges began standing in the front and shoving in the back. "Sit down," not a few mothers began to admonish the stampeding children closest around them, their smiles a bit frayed and decidedly less apologetic.

Then the mood of the crowd shifted. None of the mothers wanted their children blocked out. Instead of working to calm and sit the children down, some mothers began gesturing their children forward to get better seats; others helped maneuver theirs up to the front. The crowd began to resemble unruly fans at a soccer game.

"You stop that!" shouted one mother, pointing at my frustrated two year old, out of my reach, who had begun kicking as heedless children stepped on his hand. "We don't want boys like you here. You go home!"

Undoubtedly he had kicked her child—but she was responding like one. I watched her face snarl as she shouted at my son who in the bedlam, fortunately, didn't hear. Briefly, I found myself fighting the urge to smash in her face.

Yes, of course we were doing this for our children, but what were we doing to them? The children we hope will exhibit the best of us, easily can bring out our worst. Like a lioness defending her cub, a mother stands up for her children. Determined that they get the best, I am amazed at how easy it is for us to become aggressive and competitive.

Advertisements targeted at parents cater to this competitiveness and the underlying guilty fear that without flashcards, a mail-order reading program, or baby exercise equipment, we might be holding our child back. We buy educational toys, as if all toys don't teach children. My four year old nearly hemorrhaged with frustration after a relative gave him a math game labeled on the box as appropriate for six year olds. "I figured our family is advanced in math," I was told.

Competition can lead to some ugly behavior. Normally docile women have been known to tackle Goofy for ignoring their children at Disneyland. Little League fathers have heaped big league abuse upon umpires with whom they disagree—and that's over a game designed to teach teamwork and sportsmanship.

Even mothers do it to each other. We are masters at the art of the self-justifying put down. It alleviates our guilt. Two mothers and their children are out for dinner. One mother orders for her kids.

"I wouldn't dream of telling my children what to have," says the other mother. "They can make up their own minds."

Two mothers are talking, one works and one stays home.

"I wouldn't want strangers to raise my children," says one.

"Well, when I see my kids at the end of the day," replies the other, "I'm really happy to see them."

I have found myself playing one-up-manship as well. We are watching our children play together, my three and her one. She is pregnant with her second child and we appear to be talking about how a baby will change her life. We are really jockeying against each other for position.

"The kids will be four years apart," she says. "Like your two boys without your daughter in the middle. I'm kind of glad. My daughter is so grown up she can do things by herself now. She'll be in preschool mornings. It should work our really nicely."

"It should be easier on you," I agree. "Although four years apart is about as big a spread as I would want. Otherwise the kids don't end up being really close friends."

"Well, I remember my sisters who are 18 months apart," she counters. "They were at each other's throats constantly."

"Sure, they probably competed. That's why I'm glad I have boy-girl-boy," I agree, taking credit for something over which I have no control. "It cuts down on the competition. They fight, but they are really good friends to each other."

"I feel that I know that my daughter has had four years getting lots of attention," my friend counters. "I can tell myself she wasn't shorted in any way."

The conversation drifts away, but inside me a sense of guilt and insecurity take root. Later I ask my husband guilty questions: "Why do I feel that she was criticizing me? Do you think we have neglected our daughter? Haven't we paid enough attention to our children?"

"Hey, don't get upset," he answers. "She was just trying to justify her position and you were trying to justify yours. You haven't done anything wrong. Don't worry about it."

My husband is right, of course, and I wonder why I do. Motherhood has opened me up to the deepest feelings of insecurity I ever could have imagined. Perhaps that's because it seems so important to me to get it right. I don't want to have trouble with a fifteen year old only to discover I started making my mistakes ten years earlier. In 30 years I don't want my children to talk about me and base their concept of parenting upon how much better they can do. And so I suffer from guilt and put myself under stress. By making comparisons, I set myself up for competition.

Nobody is immune, and to an extent, we don't want to be. It's all part of caring. The trick is teaching yourself and then your child not to care so much about everything. Periodically I remind myself that before my babies were born, healthy and normal is all that I asked for. I have never heard of an employer who turned to a job applicant and asked, "So tell me, how old were you when you first learned to walk?"

9 Family Relations

THE Romans may have thrown losers to the lions, but at least the gladiators did not try to live together before they met in the arena. Two children sharing one family harbor no doubts about their combat: beating each other in the competition fondly known as sibling rivalry.

The secondborn has something the eldest did not: a sibling. A sibling is a built-in playmate, an interpreter to translate for him, and an ally his size to take his side. Siblings can be buddies, allies, or enemies. Usually, they also are rivals.

At first, parents may think it will be easy to forestall warfare in the domestic arena. They simply balance the scales in the older child's favor. A newborn doesn't feel slighted if all the time you are changing her, you also maintain a constant patter about how you admire big boys who no longer wear diapers. A baby doesn't object if, while you hold her, you also cheer her sibling at his baseball game. After about six months, however, the older one begins to realize this is another person you have brought home—not some elaborate doll that only drinks and wets. Soon the second child begins to realize something, too: somebody else got there first. Then, from the siblings' perspective, the opening salvos cannot be fired too soon.

Somehow a creeper, barely cognizant of human speech,

knows exactly how to push her big brother toward insanity. Fearlessly, she will destroy the tower he just erected, pull his hair, or pull herself to a stand in front of the television show he avidly was watching. Whatever he has, she wants. And they will wage to-the-death struggle over the same crayon, same book, or the same one of 550 identical Lego pieces.

A big brother begins to learn that Mommy comes running to the defense of a hysterically screaming baby. So he wages a more sophisticated campaign to compete with cute—as in pudgy cheeks and waddling walk. A brother's eyes become meters following the actions of his parents and other adults. They measure for exactly how long that other kid gets extra attention, and they measure how many presents each child receives and which are better. The oldest learns to take action to switch the spotlight of attention back to himself. He will do something either horrible (acting like a baby) or terrific (proving he is a big boy), depending upon whether you are having a good day or bad.

When the youngest begins throwing tantrums, the oldest monitors them closely, waiting to see whether we hang tough or give in. And I must admit the presence of a witness stiffens my spine. No more graham crackers, I say, and I'm not about to let her brother observe me slipping his sister any extra.

As time goes by, the older child reveals his true nature. He is destined for a military career of giving orders, with a minor in snitching on the side. He delights in relaying to his sister all the instructions you previously have given to him. "No, you might get hurt over there," he says—pulling her legs out from under her. ("Sorry, Mom. We had to kill the kid in order to save her.") He excels at self-righteousness. ("Mommy, she's playing inside the fireplace, but I don't know where she got the idea.")

As the children get older, rivalry takes the form of squabbling. As combat goes, it becomes more evenly matched; both children are equally irrational. We are riding home at the end of a day during which my five year old has lost all patience. He is the raw wound; his sister the salt.

"Not my house," the three year old chants after each house we pass. "Not my house, not my house, not my house."

"Be quiet," her brother shouts from the other seat. "I need peace! I want peace!"

"Not my house," she responds, barely missing a beat. If anything, she slightly turns up her volume. "Not my house, not my house." Eventually, we all need peace, but then finally it is our house and hostilities are terminated by naptime.

Like brush fires, however, they flare up again. Siblings are dry tinder in the summertime, a conflagration waiting to erupt. He asks for a snack, so I give my son one of two remaining fruit bars in the package. She asks for a snack, so I give my daughter the last remaining fruit bar in the package. She throws the empty box into the garbage. While my back is turned, war breaks out.

She throws it in the trash; he takes it out so he can throw it himself. They wrestle. He screams; she cries. Eventually Mommy—who has all the fun—takes the box and crams it into the garbage herself.

"You never let me do anything," he screams in a rage.

"I wanna do it myself," she blubbers. Before peace is restored, they are angry at me as well as each other, and I am angry at them.

As their warfare accelerated, I blamed their battles to some extent on the arrival of a new baby. The law of regression apparently follows a mathematical progression. The Terrible Twos were accompanied by the four year old Furies. I expected the two year old to start crawling again, because the four year old already had started bawling.

Peace, for example, has not broken out in the bathtub. Territorial boundaries are clearly staked in the shimmering surface of the water. My daughter gets the side by the faucet; my son the rounded end. "I want to float," she announces, stretching out her legs in a blatant incursion into his territory. "Get off of me," he screams, pounding at her toes and sending waves onto the floor.

"Take the rubber duckie out," demands my daughter, having finished with it in the bathtub.

"Are you done with it too?" I ask my son, having learned it is easier in the long run to seek permission.

"No," he says. "Keep it in the tub." OK. I put it back in the tub in my son's sovereign waters.

"Not there," he shouts, giving me a look suitable for the condemned killer of Bambi. "Over here." And he reaches across my daughter to put the duck back on her side. A malicious splash accompanies the maneuver.

"Out of the tub," she shouts.

"Over here," he shouts. "Get it off of me," he screams, once more pounding at her toes and sending waves onto the floor. And I squat there, rocking compulsively upon my heels, wondering what I have done to deserve this.

Who gets to drink the juice from the bottom of the watermelon bowl? Who got picked up first, dropped off last, or stayed up latest? Who gets dressed last or undressed first? Who throws it away, and who picks it up? First my daughter gets to turn off the television set, then we turn it back on so my son can turn it off as well. Whatever it is, if he gets one, she gets one. If she can't, he can't.

I am a mother, I continually remind myself, not a referee.

"Settle it yourselves," I demand, when they argue about who has possession of which animal sponges. "If you don't, I will pull the plug." I know I have scored a small victory for coexistence when through the bathroom door I hear them engaged in a bidding war: "I'll give you the duckie and turtle if you give me the (highly prized) lobster sponge." (Not long after this, the issue becomes moot as the two of them cooperate in chewing up the sponges.)

The magnets that mar my refrigerator doors are good for a few battles. Carefully he positions the letters in a square around the picture he painted. She comes by and moves them. "They're mine," he shouts. "No way," she insists.

We are in constant negotiations on issues as sticky as a four year old's fingers. How long can property rights be maintained over the magnets? Is possession nine-tenths of the law, or is it like leaving your purse on an empty chair before you go to the buffet line? Sometimes it is difficult for a parent not to become involved.

A typical battle might evolve like this:

"You two may play outside with your new Slinkies," I say, "while I go upstairs and put the baby to sleep for his nap. I won't be long. Nobody leaves the driveway, and nobody makes loud noise. Understand?"

Yes, affirm my five year old and my three year old, who have heard these instructions so many times they ought to have them memorized. So I can't imagine, then, why they never work.

Upstairs, I rock my toddler to sleep. An easy sort of fellow, his eyelids droop almost immediately as he accepts his destiny to snooze and miss all the fun.

"No, no, no!" Through the open window I hear my daughter bellow in a cry of rage. The toddler's eyelids flicker briefly.

"You can't do that," she screams, before her words subside into the generic wail of a cranky child.

A few minutes later I hear her reasonably quiet approach to the upstairs bedroom. As she walks up behind me, I motion her silent with a finger across my lips. As she hovers, I am not angry. Not yet. But while I weigh the relative merits of tossing the toddler into his crib before he is totally asleep, my son arrives upstairs also. Now I am aggravated.

"Mom." He hisses in the sort of stage whisper that carries into the balcony.

The toddler's eyelids fly up like a pair of window shades. Now I am angry. Ruthlessly I deposit him into his crib. Ignoring his protests, I propel his two siblings downstairs, fling them into the family room, and demand an explanation.

"What is the problem? What is so important you could not wait for me to come downstairs?" The tone of my voice indicates my usually perfect self-control has slipped slightly. Neither child wishes to draw attention to himself by answering. "Why are you fighting?" I demand.

"Well, she wouldn't let me play with my Slinky inside her circle," bleats my son, referring to the chalk circle my husband had drawn for our daughter on the driveway as he left for work that morning.

"Well, I don't want him inside my circle," whines my daughter.

There must be, I suppose, families where the bloodiest battles are reserved for matters of importance: whose turn in the bathroom, what video to rent. Not so in my family. In my family we fight about doughnut holes.

We fight about how close together we can sit in the car, and where we sit at the table. We fight over whether the bottom of one child's shoe is allowed to touch the side of the other child's chair. We patent our actions and then accuse the other party of infringement. We have turned the noun "copycat" into a verb as in: "He copycatted me." We fight, in short, over circles.

There is, however, symmetry in such preposterous behavior. Anger that inflates quickly over nothing, deflates equally as fast.

"You don't want him inside your circle?" I ask my daughter. She shakes her head warily, her finely tuned emotional radar sensing a trap.

"Well, I'll fix that," I snarl as I drag them both outside to the offending sidewalk. Grabbing the chalk, I proceed to draw a second circle.

"There. Now you each have your own."

Dumbly my children look at me as if I have just told them the bathtub is really a spaceship. They look at the circles, look at their Slinkies, and then look at each other. Silently, they reach a mutual decision. Without looking at me, they both head inside the house. Outside, obviously, there's nothing fun left to do.

When it comes to fighting, clearly no ant hill is too small to be made into a mountain. We fight over rollie-pollie bugs as well as ants. One day, my son set a record of sorts. "She's looking at me," he shrieked, pointing to his sister.

Parents are placed in a precarious role. You must tread the fine line between allowing children to resolve conflicts on their own, and your desire to have them both reach adulthood. You must fortify yourself to be less fearful and less watchful than the first time around, lest you become the referee in every fight. One mother has a rule she will intervene only when she sees blood. You may spend more time litigating property rights than an attorney. And you may end up buying two of a lot of items.

You learn to create chores that are separate but equally

desirable. If one child opens the front gates, you will learn to make sure the other gets to carry the key to the door. If you send one child to empty the dryer, the other gets to reload it. And if you have kisses for one, you must have hugs for the other.

The issue, of course, isn't so much whether both kids get everything the same, but rather that each gets what he needs. Fairness, I theorize, is not the same as equality. The issue is not to give each child the same amounts, but rather enough of anything he or she needs. I refuse to buy new shoes for two when only one pair of feet has grown. You may be dealing with one child who wants to read a book that the other child wants to chew. Knowing this, however, why do I find myself counting the number of peas I put on each plate at dinner? Why do I make sure always to give everyone the same color vitamin each day? The answer is easy. Because I don't know how else to avoid the solution: giving them both my personal and undivided attention.

Then, for a while, I was deluded into believing five years old marked the dawn of the age of reason. When I would request "wait a minute," my son actually would wait. My son appeared to be developing patience and perspective. Now I see that was all delusion. Instead of my daughter learning maturity from my son, he is learning immaturity from her. Sometimes it is impossible to tell where their squabbling ends and tantrums begin. She screams because I presumed to help her take off her pants. A few minutes later my son screams because his arms got stuck and he cannot quite take off his shirt. Then he screams at her because she won't stop screaming, and he screams at me for trying to help.

Of course it's not all bad. To some extent I have learned to exploit their Punch-and-Judy relationship.

"Come take your medicine," I tell the three year old, reminding her in a stage whisper that her brother can't have any. "When you were a baby you used to scream just like that about putting your pajamas on," I tell the five year old as I help him into his.

And, sometimes, I see humor in the situation. We are brushing teeth before bedtime.

"I want water," she demands.

"You need to ask nicely," I admonish, reminding her and anyone else who will listen that slavery is outlawed. "It's not: 'I want water.' It's: 'May I please have some water?'"

"Yes, Mommy," she smiles. "You can."

But some of the time I don't have the perspective to step back and laugh. One time I requested my son's help with the laundry.

"Please put all the socks together in a pile," I said.

"This is no fun," he informed me after a minute, abandoning the job.

"I know," I replied. "I don't like it either, but it has to get done."

"Well, you do it."

"Well, how about I don't do it and we just let the clothes stay dirty, or, we can all do our own." (My tone of voice is strictly rational.)

"No," he shouted. "The boss always has to do more work. And I don't like this conversation. I don't want to be in it."

Shortly thereafter, when he asked me to read him a story, I declined to reward him until after dinner. He screamed about this for a while. At dinner, when I put vegetables on his plate, he screamed even more. He didn't want them. I'd had it. And in one moment of intense satisfaction, I regressed.

"All right," I screamed. "You don't have to eat them!" And

I flung the carrots in his face where, briefly, he wore them. Then, being the adult that I am, I proceeded to mop up the floor.

OCCASIONALLY, however, parents remember why they had more than one child. I once saw my son take his sister for a walk. When the two held hands, they fit together like the pieces of a puzzle. I want my children to be friends. Sometimes, that's exactly what they are.

If anyone had asked me to describe the relationship of my two oldest children, I would have said they are like driftwood. Take them outside, offer them a selection of friends to choose from, and I would have predicted they would go their separate ways. Occasionally they would be snagged at the same spot, but generally they would glide past each other to their own destinations. I would have made this assumption based on past experience at home. When they are together, they fight. Presumably two children who excel at mutual taunting and torture have no use for each other. Presumably they cannot wait to get away from each other. Presumably they cannot stand each other, and if only they didn't have to share a bedroom, a bathroom, and a family together, they wouldn't be—together, that is.

Not so. When they began to attend the same preschool together, I found out that my children cannot bear to be apart.

The first clue I had is when they came home and told me it was not fair one of them had potato chips and the other corn chips in their respective lunch boxes. The next night, when my daughter informed me she spilled the milk in her thermos, my son informed me it was all right because he wiped it up. "Tomorrow, I'll teach her how to pour better," he confided.

There are 35 children at this school, and somehow I never expected my two would sit next to each other. But that's not all. When I asked my daughter if she slept at nap time, my son informed me that she had. I asked him how he knew. "I took her in to nap because she didn't want to go with the teacher," he said. "And I checked later. She was asleep."

When I come to pick the two of them up, almost always I find them playing with the same group of children. And if they are not together, their antennae are twitching and they can tell me precisely where the other one is. The teachers tell me my son is protective of his younger sister. He wants to know why she is crying, where she is going, and if she is in trouble.

True, I sense his attentions are motivated not only by concern but by a desire to mount a police action. He exults, no doubt, in the fact that his sister has to nap but he does not. When my daughter asked her teacher to rip open the foil package around her granola bar, my son evidently sprang up to be of assistance. Turns out he also was checking to make sure she had eaten her sandwich first. Still, for a while at least, my daughter was flattered. She had to be cajoled each morning into joining her class. At three years old, she seemed to think her rightful place was in the classroom with her five year old brother. And recently, when one of my son's chums sent an invitation to his birthday party, I was nonplussed to see it came addressed to my daughter as well.

This is heartening news, that my kids can't stand each other only in private. But at home it isn't always private. There's Mom and Dad. And already I can sense their new-found alliance can give rise to an us-versus-them mentality. The other day, after the two had driven each other to distraction, my husband had had enough. He came out swinging after the two of them.

"Quick!" My daughter held open the door and motioned

her brother inside. "Come in," she shouted. "I'll help you. Don't let him get you." Apparently, nothing cements friendship faster than the presence of a mutual enemy.

DESPITE my entreaties to tone it down, the two children have wrestled their way from good-natured laughter into outraged hysterics. I try to administer justice tempered by mercy. "You get on the couch," I order my son. "You over on the chair," I tell my daughter. My husband attends to our son; I turn to our daughter. I give her a hug, but her body stiffens under mine. She wriggles free. "I want Daddy," she cries and flees to the couch where the three of them engage in a veritable love fest without me. Feeling about as useful as a bicycle to a baby, I go upstairs and wait to be noticed. Even the baby, asleep, doesn't need me.

Eventually, when his stomach announces it's time for dinner, my son comes seeking me out. "Mommy," he asks, "why did you go upstairs?"

"Because nobody wanted me downstairs," I answer honestly.

"Oh, Mommy," he tells me, "we all want you."

I know that, of course, but nevertheless it is good to hear.

Just as siblings can be rivals with each other for their parents' attention, parents can also be rivals with each other for their children's affections.

Children are like planets. Periodically they fall into orbit under the gravitational pull of one particular parent to the exclusion of the other. I can gauge my relative popularity by how many children choose to hold my hand when we are crossing the street with Daddy. During those times it is good to remember that Daddy's Girl today will want to wear nail polish with Mommy tomorrow. Babies are the only children to give sole custody of their affections to Mommy—and that can last only briefly until they realize anyone can hold a bottle.

Affections are most likely to be alienated, I've noticed, when one parent is missing. The parent who remains is common as dirt; the one gone instantly is elevated to sainthood. When my husband is out of town, the children know the family is incomplete. Each night we recite catechism as they ask how many more mornings they must wake up without him. Even the baby knows that Daddy is gone. He does not have the words to ask, but periodically he will gaze at the front door quizzically, as if wondering why one of us is missing. In the same way, he fusses at nighttime when I am not in the room, because he knows I am the one who puts him to sleep. He isn't ready to sleep yet, but he is reassured to know that I am available when he needs me. Children are like that.

When my children are angry at me, they want their Daddy. When they are angry at him, they want their Mommy. When our son has a nightmare, he wants his father's reassurance that black spiders are not coming out of the sheets to get him. When our daughter fusses about brushing her teeth, she cries at her father: "I want Mommy to do it." In tandem, in balance, we are their ballasts. Apart, the family is out of balance.

My husband and I are not rivals, but sometimes it is tempting to try to score points at your partner's expense—especially when a child comes running in tears, taking his case to the court of appeals. My husband lays down the law to our daughter; she runs to me for comfort. I tell our son to be quiet and sit still; he takes his hurt feelings to Daddy's side of the room. We must restrain ourselves so we don't fall into a good-guy-bad-guy routine.

In the end, of course, I am glad I have two boys and a girl. It triples the odds that at least one child at any given time will like me. It's not that children prefer one parent to another. It's just that sometimes they want to copy the parent of whom they are a replica, and other times they want to flirt with the parent of whom they are not. When Daddy does macho chores around the house involving manly activities like hammering, making noise, and making a mess, my son is eager to fetch and carry. When Mommy is putting on makeup, my daughter demands a turn to try some on. (She's disappointed I don't wear more.)

I know I will always share a sisterhood with my daughter. She is my ally in a male household, and someday she also may grow up to be a mother. It is with her father, however, that she flirts. When my daughter bats her eyes trying to coax a forbidden ice cream bar, she aims her glances at Daddy.

Likewise, my relationship with my sons will be different. Only a boy can court his mother's heart. When I get dressed up to go steppin' out, my son approaches shyly to tell me I look beautiful. I remember the time my son won a party game and chose as his prize a bottle of perfume for me. It was the color of a laboratory specimen and reeked of the lilies of a million fields. I didn't like the scent, but I wanted to bottle the look on his face as he handed it to me. I anointed myself with the stuff on the spot, and I keep it in a special place—right next to my macaroni necklaces.

YOU look like a mother, you act like a mother. Your husband calls you Mom even when the children cannot hear. You must be somebody's mother. There is, in fact, only one time during which you may not feel like a mother—and that is when you are talking to yours. There is nothing like a visiting mother, aunt, or cousin to turn your sense of authority on its ear.

Sometimes, feeling like a child again can bother you. When the generations are rivals for supremacy, some houses turn out to be big enough to hold only one mother.

Although she has never said so, I can sense that my mother does not understand about nursing babies. A modern mother of the fifties, she fed her babies the latest thing: formula. As I feed my babies the oldest thing, I can sense she does not understand the rationale that prompts me to nurse any longer than she thinks I have to. "Are you still nursing?" she asks. Implied in her tone of voice she means: Isn't it long enough? Don't you want to use something sanitary to feed that baby, like a bottle? (My mother, who is by no means prissy, frowns upon dipping the peanut butter knife in the jelly jar.)

The changes in child-rearing techniques over the last 30 years are enough to pit the generations against each other. The pediatrician credits you with enough sense to follow his directions; your own relatives may not. It's only natural. To them, those directions sound like nothing they have ever heard before.

Fresh from my classes on natural childbirth, straight out of a birthing center, my labor and delivery had little in common with my own mother's. The generations divide neatly over the issue of whether a father ought to be present at the birth of his child. The current crop of grandparents finds even the photographs of birth distasteful; they do not look upon the actual experience as a spectator event.

To a generation nurtured on belly binders, bottles, and baby nurses, the way we do things today seems startling. My relatives used to wonder why I was not yet feeding my baby cereal. They thought me slightly dense when I then presumed to wonder why he wasn't yet sleeping through the night. "Some rice cereal in his bottle will take care of that," I've heard them say. When I tell the sales clerk to fit my toddler in sneakers, my mother-in-law asks him to bring a pair of leather high tops. As I tell my son to "use his words," or sentence my three year old to "time out" after she sasses me, I can see grandparents giving me fish eyes. I know all about the new theories of child-rearing, their looks say, but in my day a good crack on the bottom did the trick.

Your own mother, in short, may be the slowest to treat you like a mother instead of a daughter. Your mother-in-law is likely to make the switch quite quickly. Immediately she will stop telling you how to take care of her son—and concentrate on advising you about her grandchildren.

For such relatives, extended visits with your children are a great treat. Just as flowers thrive on sunshine, they need to bask in the children often. Usually they are good sports—sharing a bathroom with a five year old is never easy. When they come to see the children, however, they also see the parents. Playing host at the same time you are playing parent can strain the fabric of an already full household.

Sometimes relatives are simply out of synch. We are engaged in a crash program to build up big brother's ego—at the same time grandpa gushes on about how cute his little sister is. We are emphasizing to little sister how she is big enough to be a big sister—at the same time grandma keeps calling her a good baby. We are downplaying competition to our son—at the same time a cousin admires his picture as the best in his class.

When the extended family is extended across the country, a visiting relative can nag at you like a loose thread you're dying to pull. This is so, I believe, because children pose the challenge of a Rorschach ink blot test. Parents and relatives look at the same thing and see something entirely different, but with equal intensity. Many grandmas fundamentally want to keep their grandchildren little. Such grandmas relish hugs and cuddly little bodies. Every offer to read a story is preceded by the request "Come sit on my lap." They mourn the passing of dependency with as much fervor as a mother relishes the independence that means a two year old actually can entertain herself for more than five minutes.

A visiting relative subconsciously believes normal rules should be suspended during his visit. A mother firmly believes sticking to the schedule is all that stands between her and insanity. After a week of late dinners, delayed naps, and abandoned bedtimes, some visitors have yet to figure out why the kids are cranky and Mom is getting irritable. Even the relatives who say they don't want to upset the schedule inevitably do. They finally seem ready to embark on the day's outing about 20 minutes before naptime. Long after the fact, I still hadn't forgiven one visitor for running the disposal in the kitchen for a lemon peel when she knew I was upstairs trying to rock a cranky child to sleep.

Visiting relatives suffer severe allergies to tears. They want nothing to do with disciplining a child; that is a stain they prefer to leave on somebody else's hands. In fact, they frequently function as defense attorney for a youngster by explaining why whatever happened wasn't really the child's fault. Parents, who believe even cute kids can do ugly things, tend to see this as undercutting their authority.

Visiting relatives are driven to a kind of desperation about their temporary status, trying to win permanent residency in the children's hearts. Several times I have handed the telephone to a child only to have him audibly ask: "Now, what's his name I'm talking to?" We try to rehearse the children before a visit, hauling out the photo album to remind them exactly who is coming. Desperation still gives rise to what I call the I-Won't-Rush-Them Syndrome. It's when the relatives swear they will take it easy and wait to win acceptance—and then within the first 20 minutes they end up mugging the toddler, desperate for kisses.

Of course children enjoy the commotion of having visitors in the house. Mine stampede downstairs each morning to check out the guest room to see if anyone fled overnight. Sadly, just about the time the kids remember by themselves to kiss So-and-So goodnight, the house is "empty" because the guests have boarded a plane back home. The biggest drawback to visiting relatives, of course, is the very fact that they are visiting. They are neither here long enough to call for permanent adjustments, nor for them to feel an integral part of the family. The solution to the problem, I recognize, is obvious: Make them visit even more often for longer periods. But for reasons equally obvious, I don't always want to suggest it.

10 Husband Is the Past Tense of Daddy

YOU remember your husband. He was the guy with whom you used to hold uninterrupted conversations. You used to hold some of them when the two of you went out for dinner—in the middle of the week, on the spur of the moment, at restaurants where they don't have a kids' menu. And while you sat there (dining, not eating), the two of you might discuss how both your jobs were going or what part of the house you were planning to remodel next. Possibly you talked about where you were thinking of heading for your next vacation.

You didn't plan that vacation around the times when school was out. You didn't pick your neighborhood on the basis of its school system, and you didn't hesitate to buy a white couch.

You didn't have children then. You didn't whine and dine. It was a time when you celebrated only your anniversary; not Father's Day. The former marks your time together as a couple; the latter can acknowledge the end of it. My husband and I were married for eight years before we became parents. Friends ask if I'm glad we waited so long, and I say absolutely. Marriage is like a bank account. For eight years we made steady deposits; right now we can afford to make a few withdrawals.

Sometime after wives give birth to babies, their husbands give way to daddies. A husband and wife will never look at each other in the same way again. What they see can be better for the family than it is for the marriage. Becoming parents sends a husband and wife on the start of a wonderful journey; the rest of your life you are bonded together by pride in the children you have created. But if children bring you closer together as parents, that's not necessarily what they do for you as husband and wife.

If the children come first, sometimes the marriage needs to come in a closer second. My husband sometimes forgets that the mother of his children also is his wife. This means he now shops for our anniversary in the drug store because our son reminded him to buy me something. Instead of falling asleep holding my hand, he holds the TV control box.

Rather than feeling romantic, some days my strongest emotion is immense gratitude that my husband is in this with me. He can't come back another time when the children are less grumpy or walk out the door if the noise level is deafening. When the going gets tough, he can't quit in disgust and tell me: "I don't do children." When he walks through the door each night, I welcome him as another pair of hands. If I say, "The baby is hungry and your daughter skipped her nap," I don't have to explain. He automatically knows this means we have a rough night ahead. So he takes off his tie with one hand as he turns on the bath water with the other.

Parenting turns the partnership of marriage into the teamwork of an athletic event. With small children, days can become marathon events. Taking care of everyone is like a relay race: You and your husband constantly are handing off to each other. Sometimes it doesn't leave much for each other. Gratitude does not a romance make.

Nurturing a marriage in the face of young children requires the three Ps: privacy, passion, and persistence. They can be hard to muster. Privacy is impossible. Children do more than fill previously empty bedrooms. They have filled my bedroom with all the activity of a train station. At all hours of the night, there are arrivals and departures. Sick children, frightened children, and just plain lonely children come for a visit and sometimes stay the night. My husband and I switched to a king-sized mattress. "We need it," he jokes, "to sleep a family of five."

When we decide to take a stab at passion, we need to arrange privacy. The easiest way is to wait until the children are all asleep. By then, of course, usually we are too. Many a Saturday night, after I put the baby to sleep at 9, I am the last one in the household left awake. This is because most mornings no one lingers in bed past 7 A.M. (Children do not take weekends off.) So passion is also a function of energy.

But for what we lack in energy we sometimes compensate in creativity. It requires persistence. The VCR, I had discovered, offers the biggest bang for the buck in terms of buying times for ourselves. Back in the olden days when we had only one child, I can remember plopping him into the wind-up swing so we could enjoy a few minutes alone. But every time that swing would stop, he would begin to scream. It was one of the few times I have ever wished we had the battery-operated model of anything.

I thought about all this one day when I saw a couple sitting together at the park. They were a matched set, four legs stretched out and crossed at the ankles as they slouched in companionable ease on a bench watching the children. Her head rested on his shoulder; his arm was draped across her back.

The more I watched them as I pushed my daughter on the swing, the more my irritation—or was it envy?—began to grow. First, in an area bustling with early morning activity, they were inert and at ease. And second, in a place usually the weekday domain of mothers and children, they were together behaving like lovers.

I couldn't help but contrast their behavior to the last time my husband and I took our children to the park. We enjoyed family fun, not to be confused with a date. My husband flew a kite, while our son unwound all the string. We applauded our daughter on her way down the twisty slide as we pushed the baby on the swing. We rode our bikes home and raced to see who could reach the corner first. But my husband and I never held hands, much less sat on the bench and slouched together. We rarely were even side by side.

We've arranged our lives around our children. I know households, for example, where dinner is served at 5 P.M., long before Daddy's arrival but right about when the kids are hungry. The parents eat alone together later, after the children's baths. In my household, baths come before dinner. Dinner is at 7 P.M., after Daddy arrives and long after the children are ready to eat. Noisy, chaotic, and confusing though it might be, dinner is our family time. At least once a day we are all together and we all share in the same conversation. I believe that if we didn't all sit down together at least once a day, we might need to be re-introduced the next time we assemble.

But as the couple in the park unintentionally pointed out to me, much more rarely are my husband and I ever alone. There are couples who can hold meaningful conversations after the children are asleep. When we remain awake that late, my husband and I are not among them. And we tend to discuss things like the car insurance in the mornings when my husband is on his way out of the shower and I am on my way in.

Before my third child was born, my neighbor offered me a present: one night of babysitting. I reminded her that she babysat for me once before, two years earlier. After my daughter was born, she had taken care of my son while my husband came to the hospital to join me for dinner on my last night.

"Surely that wasn't the last time you two went out to dinner alone," she exclaimed. I had to pause and think for a minute before reassuring her that it wasn't. The last movie we watched together at the theater, however, was *Bambi*.

Of course, I know all about the theory: To keep a marriage successful you need to date your mate. And I know that we intend to. It's just that we've been busy, having three children in five years. In a sense we've put our marriage down right now, hoping that when we get back, it still will be right where we left it. If we are practicing emotional triage, I guess we have chosen to devote our energies to the children before the couple.

And I also know about the danger of trying to resuscitate a marriage: Wait too long and some day in 20 years when you finally sit down alone at the dinner table, you and your husband will realize you have nothing left to say to each other unless you talk about the children. I remember the families of my childhood where the parents divorced after their children graduated high school. As a child I was surprised by what happened in those seemingly happy families; as an adult I understand.

So I guess that's why I was irritated with the couple at the park. They had come to a mecca for family fun and had chosen to flaunt themselves as a couple. And I guess that's why I kept an eye on them, curious to see how many of their children they had ignored that morning at the park while they spent their time with each other. And I have to admit that I felt a whole lot better when eventually I watched them get up and leave the park with none.

CHILDREN change the criterion by which husbands and wives evaluate each other. Your husband's previous attraction for you as a smooth dancer or sweet-talker can end up counting far less than his survival skills: how fast he can give baths or take away uncapped magic markers. Just as women learn to be mothers, men learn to be daddies. But we learn to excel at very different skills. If women aren't careful, their husbands learn to let them take care of the children.

When we got married, my husband and I were a liberated couple—in principle and on paper. We drew up an agreement to share daily chores equitably. I cooked; he washed dishes. I dusted; he vacuumed. We both did laundry. But, somehow, in practice it never quite felt equitable to me.

While he washed the dinner dishes, I would be fixing the next day's lunches. He would vacuum all right, but only after I reminded him. When it came to the laundry, I sorted the loads, and each time I had to tell him how to set the machine. We both folded, but although I knew where everything went in his dresser, he left my clothes piled on top of mine.

I should have read the future in the tea leaves of my underwear. Instead, I had a baby. When our son was born, we both went to the hospital class on giving baths. "If you learn when I do," I said, "then you'll know as much as I do. I don't want to be the expert while you watch." But as it turned out, the wet baby was slippery and he was nervous. So was I, but I managed.

My husband was an involved first-time father. He would

play with his son and change his diaper whenever I asked. Since I nursed, he couldn't feed the baby at first, but even later he continued to watch as I taught the baby to eat solids. Since I was home on maternity leave, I had the time to deal with the pediatrician and locate baby-sitters.

So I became competent first. He knew I was his safety net, his backup, the one responsible for all the new duties at home. He relied on me. I can remember once asking him to give the baby his medicine. My husband, holding the clearly labeled prescription bottle, turned to me and asked: "Now, how much of this does he get?" Gradually, it dawned on me that previously he had known how to read. It wasn't just that he wouldn't assume responsibility, or that he couldn't; somehow he didn't.

Eventually, the Competency Factor came into play. I got to be better at running the household and taking charge of the baby, so I got to do it. Then, the Criticism Factor came into play. When he did help out, I functioned like a coach, shouting instructions from the sidelines: "Use the ointment, not the powder; cut the pieces smaller; there's a shirt that matches those pants; remember his vitamins." To this day, my husband has no idea how our children's clothes are organized in their drawers. They remain as much a mystery to him as mine do.

I didn't like having to tell him what to do. He didn't like being told. It began to feel easier just to do it all because then I felt like less of a nag. I got everything done on my schedule. My husband felt less nagged, but gradually he also began to feel my resentment because he wasn't helping out. The baby began to learn: Mommy was in charge of food, naps, and meals. When Daddy came home it was time for fun. My husband's triumphant appearance each evening, when it was time to play with a bathed and pajama-clad boy just before bedtime, annoyed me.

But when I did adopt a take-your-turn attitude, he didn't do everything as efficiently as I did. When he babysat, I had to steel myself for the mess before I walked in the door. I can do the dishes and keep the toys picked up, I would fume, why can't he? I'm not sure whether I learned to play my role, or he learned to play his. We had redivided our division of labor, but it still didn't feel even. I recognized ourselves in an exchange I witnessed at the neighbors'. They have a toy closet in the alcove under the stairs.

"I just love it because I just throw the toys inside," the husband said, illustrating how his wife had gone overboard. "I throw them in, but she's a little crazy. She comes back and organizes them all." He smiled as he said this; his wife didn't.

Dissatisfaction didn't stop me from having a second child, and in a way it helped me to get even—if only for a few days. While I recovered in the hospital, my husband was home all by himself taking care of our son. Somehow, he managed to dress our son in his clothes—although he did not find time to wash them.

With each child, my husband's level of involvement and competence has increased. Needless to say, it is never enough to satisfy me. Just as many women find themselves assuming their mothers' roles, many men find themselves behaving like their fathers. Mothers-in-law might not agree, but such behavior is not necessarily a mark of progress. Mothers-in-law tend to think their sons are doing more than their husbands ever did. Wives often think their own husbands need to do much more.

Many fathers don't seem to be as intimately involved in the nitty gritty of their children's lives. How many men helped select the pediatrician or remember on their own to give a child his medicine? How many men know what size diaper the baby wears or what size pants the oldest wears? How many men are first to notice when a pair of shoes becomes too small? How many men can correctly dress their children in appropriate clothes? How many men plan the guest list for a birthday party? How many men are the first to stay home with a sick child? And how many men have authority to authorize afternoon snack?

Men must have natural antibodies against noticing much of the world around them. It's a form of mental immunity, possibly a trait genetically linked to males. I can see how my son already has inherited it from his father:

It had been a rough week, and I was lying on the bed trying to nap. One child is asleep; the other two are watching a movie in the room with me. My husband stops by to ask if there's anything he can do. "Clean up the kitchen," I say before drifting off.

Dimly I hear the doorbell ring, and vaguely I realize my son has brought his friend upstairs to watch the movie and watch me sleep. They play with the baby. Suddenly, all is silence and I pass out. I emerge uneasily from a dream about how the kids are walking on the roof, to hear the baby whimpering in the playpen for somebody to pay him attention. Taking him downstairs, I find the kids raiding the refrigerator and my husband nowhere to be found. Tracking him down eventually, I ask: "Couldn't you keep an eye on things? Couldn't you let me sleep?"

"Sorry," comes his brilliant rejoinder. "I didn't know you were sleeping."

A few days later the baby is sleeping and his brother is playing quietly in the same room. Suddenly, I hear the squeaker toy on the baby's crib sounding reveille right over his head. Sprinting at top speed to admonish my son not to wake up the baby, I find I am too late. The infant who should have slept for another hour is awake and peering about. "Why did you wake him up?" I shout. "Why didn't you just let him sleep?"

"I didn't notice he was sleeping," comes my son's brilliant rejoinder. Sometimes a child's brilliance is merely a reflection of his parent's candle power.

NOW I must admit, my husband is amiable. He will do what-ever chore I specifically ask, eventually. But as one disgruntled wife told her husband: "I'm not the tour guide here. If you live here, then you should know without asking what needs to be done." Even so, most men have tremendous capacity to ignore. They can ignore the overwhelming evidence contained within a diaper. They can play with a baby, hold that baby, and pass him back to Mommy without smelling a thing. Their nose doesn't work.

Men, in short, are tempting targets for husband bashing—a sport easily overrated because it holds no challenge. Fathers—especially the kind who cannot distinguish at 20 paces between a medium and a large diaper—offer too big a target for the cheap shot. When I was in labor the third time, for example, my husband was right there beside me. He was finishing up paperwork from the office. Hours after our son was born, he told me that he felt a lot better—because he really had needed to get that report finished.

Once when I asked my husband to clean up the kitchen, he ran the dishwasher for five glasses. Then, when I bellowed about how that wasn't really what I had in mind, he attempted to persuade me that the appliance used less water than the sink. Now you know exactly what kind of husband he is. By confiding a few secrets, I can reduce my husband with ridicule and find out he shares his lowest common denominator with plenty of other fathers. Other mothers have told me: Our husbands must be twins separated at birth.

Many men suffer from blind spots. They can watch a football game while stretched out on the couch, blissfully unaware that the rocking horse is about to defy the laws of gravity, or that every sock formerly in the drawer now decorates the floor. Likewise, when my husband would take our son to preschool, he would sign him in on the sheet positioned beneath the bulletin board. Posted on that board were notices of such crucial information as staff names and school rules. This same husband once asked me how I knew the names of all the teachers. He never saw the signs. Some men, who for years have been hearing their wives without listening, go totally deaf. They won't hear two children in a death struggle for possession of the same book if it occurs while the news is on.

Ironically, as a father's senses break, mommy's seem to work better than ever. Even in their sleep, mothers can determine whether a cry means serious business or just a restless sleep. We can hear the crinkle of a package of cookies being opened downstairs in the kitchen. And without looking, a mommy knows who hit first and senses when the crayon is about to make contact with the wall.

Mothers feel a greater moral obligation to entertain their children. If an empty day looms ahead, mothers are the ones trying to fill it with activities to keep the kids busy. Dads feel no such obligation and are likely to adopt a more laissez-faire approach. Whereas a mother will pick up a book and read with the children, a father is more apt to turn on the television so they can watch together. I've heard several mothers lament:

Quality time is not time spent watching TV. Men don't keep track when it comes to quality time. They just assume it will happen.

Fathers are better at shutting things out and totally relaxing. A mother doesn't come off duty until the children are asleep. Mothers, for example, are constitutionally unable to indulge in or ignore a good mess. They are the ones sweeping the sand back into the sandbox or craning under the bed for the missing puzzle pieces. Fathers easily co-exist with chaos. Might as well take every toy out of the closet, a father figures, before worrying about picking any of them up. Fathers are more likely to think letting the kids dig in the dirt is OK, partly because they are blissfully unaware that the children are wearing their good clothes.

This difference of style nowhere is illustrated more clearly than in a man's ability to immerse himself in a project. A man will decide to make something and, by golly, that is what he will do. As he works for hours on end, it becomes a woman's job to entertain the children and keep them out of his tools. I realize all individuals are subject to imperatives. For little boys it is a primordial urge to dig. For little girls it is the need to color rainbows. For toddlers it is an involuntary impulse to climb. For big boys, also known as men, it is the project imperative. The only thing a man loves more than embroiling himself in a project is watching another man work on his project.

In my household my husband's most recent project has been building an overgrown cycle eight feet long with six wheels and seats for nine. Not many families can claim to have a hexacycle in their garage, but then, not many families need one. We have no need, either, but that did not deter my husband who designed and built the vehicle. For the past year, this has been his weekend project, his creative outlet. Midnight finds him spoking wheels in the garage; weekends find him taking innumerable trips to the hardware store. He spends more time shopping for the parts he needs than I do shopping for a bathing suit. He has cornered the market on bicycle chains.

I have nothing against the contraption, but I see it as a symbol of all that differentiates a father from a mother. Fathers undertake hobbies and projects because they want to; mothers rarely make it to that point of thinking about themselves. The husbands in our neighborhood, excited by the hexacycle, check regularly to see how it is coming; the wives give me sympathetic smiles.

Show me a parent who naps when the children are not asleep, and I will show you a father. On the list of things I most want my husband to take care of around the house, the cycle would finish dead last. It is, however, a male trait to block out the demands of those around him when a man decides to think of himself. I am jealous every time I hear of a father gone fishing with the boys. I tell myself that compared to me, such men surely are less efficient, but I also suspect their mental health is stronger than mine.

It must be a different genetic trait that prevents me from putting my feet up with a book if the dishes are dirty. I never met a man who had it (the trait, not the big feet). I'm not saying that a woman's approach is better. But I am saying a woman's approach is different.

I have seen my husband give our son ice cream for snack, knowing full well he refused to eat lunch.

"We don't eat ice cream until after lunch," I lecture him.

"Well," my husband explains, "he said he didn't want lunch."

I have gone out, leaving three children and a husband in their pajamas. When I return hours later, everyone has been playing, but nobody is dressed.

I tell myself that when my husband opens a new milk carton without noticing the one already open, his inattention to detail is not a manifestation of evil. I tell myself that when he opens a bottle of cranberry juice because he's sick of the apple juice already in there, he is not being bad. I only know that a mother would never consider opening a new bottle for herself before the old one is finished.

"Dad wants to work on the hexacycle," my son informs me with an inherited sense of excitement.

"Dad should fix the garage door," I respond with noticeable lack of enthusiasm.

My son gives me a quizzical glance.

"We're having a disagreement," I explain, "about what Daddy should do."

"Oh," chimes in my daughter. "You're having a fight, just like the Berenstain Bears."

Sort of. In the book, Brother and Sister Bear kiss and make up.

To children, of course, Dad is more often a hero and Mom a nag. Children evaluate parents by different criteria. Every kid in the neighborhood can ride on a bicycle built for nine. Nobody lines up to see a clean kitchen. For this reason, fathers generally are more fun than mothers. Sure, they may be called upon for heavy-duty discipline, as in wait until your father gets home, but they also are more likely to be found rough-housing on the floor, doubling as a jungle gym or trampoline. Fathers also are more likely to initiate such activities before bedtime—thereby revving up the motors to the engines mothers are eager to shut down. More than a few mothers, in fact, have been known to mutter that the schedule seems to flow more smoothly when Dad isn't home.

But that is also the point: Most dads aren't home as much as moms. They are less intimately involved in their children's daily lives. Not always there during prime time, Dad misses some of the golden moments. His nightly arrival engenders excitement, but a child who babbled endlessly about preschool at lunchtime, by dinnertime barely can remember that he had been there at all. Children have a way of letting Dad know he's been working too many hours. One morning, after his father had worked late the night before, our son, then three, asked without rancor: "Did you come home to visit?"

Most fathers are apt to come home from work during what one mother calls the Suicide Hour. This is when you are coping with cranky children who were ready to eat an hour ago. This is the time even the most agreeable baby is apt to cry. In my household, the Suicide Hour usually starts when I simultaneously am giving baths upstairs and cooking dinner downstairs. While they wait for Dad and a well-done dinner, the kids pass the time trying to kill each other. For this reason, no matter how late he arrives, Dad is welcome as a fresh reinforcement for Mom and a fresh face to the kids. Then he's usually jumped on, yelled at, or put to work before he takes off his tie.

Nightly, Dad displays his courage by walking through the front door. He knows that although he missed the beginning of the fight and nobody can establish why everyone is screaming, his job will be to stop it. No matter how much abuse we heap on him, each night Daddy comes back for more. He loves us, and he lives there and knows that so long as there are growing children in the house, he will always get fed.

In all fairness, however, I will give my husband credit; I just don't believe I owe him. I rely on my husband to hold up his end—just as he assumes I will hold up mine. He helps, but so he should. If he feels heroic, maybe it's not because he does so much, but perhaps because other husbands admit to doing so little. Less than perfect though his efforts might be, I suspect some men wouldn't even match them.

Sometimes, my husband truly is heroic. Instead of always scoring points against him, I must confess he has at times earned a few. He must be a help because when he's gone, there's so much more to do.

I used to believe taking care of three children all day was a man's job for which only a mother is qualified. But then I remember the time we all went on vacation together. It was a lot of work. Anyone who has ever spent two nights in one hotel room with three children will understand. When the five year old and the three year old locked both doors to the bathroom in our room and then proceeded to slam them shut, my husband was the one who used the nail scissors to pop the locks. When my legs gave out at the bottom of the tropical rain forest at the San Diego Zoo, my husband was the one who carried our daughter in a backpack and pushed the baby in his stroller up an incline so steep the air was thin. When our son lay his head down on my lap as our ship sailed toward Catalina Island, and then barfed all over me, my husband was the one who brought paper towels. And when at brunch first our son and then our daughter spilled orange juice all over the restaurant table, my husband was the one who wiped it up and then wore juice all over his pants.

I remember the time I challenged him to either fold laundry or to exercise with me. My husband was the one who fell to the floor breathless first and questioned whether the video had been doctored, or whether such contortions actually were attainable by the human body. He may not be in top athletic shape, but my husband is a good sport. He allows me to chide him. He also recognizes that until he can do everything my way, I will never consider him perfect.

🕭

WHEN my husband comes home from the office, he likes to change his clothes and wash up first thing. After he is refreshed, then he likes to watch the evening news before sitting down to dinner. Many is the day when I won't let him get away with it.

Because I know Dad is not just a temporary pinch hitter, I constantly push him to pull his weight on the team. Petty, yes, but if I am not able to sit down and relax, neither is he. I suggest, snarl, and otherwise orchestrate his movements so that he helps out. He has no right to read the mail if it's time for baths. "Go ask Daddy," I tell my daughter when she requests juice while I am holding the baby and serving dinner. He's just standing there, my tone of voice implies in a private message to my husband.

Yet despite my actions (or perhaps because of them), my husband has perfected a typically male and extremely effective technique for work avoidance. He goes upstairs after dinner, lies down on the bed, and falls asleep. When I am feeling particularly ruthless, I have been known to send a child up to wake him.

All of this is part of what I call The Continuing Quest To Make Fathers Do Their Share. Nowhere has my push been more ferocious, the battle more protracted, than when it comes to enlisting help in the mornings getting everyone out of the house. Like my husband, I also have had an office to which I was required to report at an approximate time each morning. After three years of taking care of our two children myself, finally it occurred to me that my husband could share the chore. I backed my husband up against the wall and into an egalitarian corner. What modern man is going to go on record as saying that he's not willing to do his fair share? And so it began.

For Daddy, the experience of taking charge was an eye-opener. He told me how much he enjoyed the time together with his son and daughter almost as often as he told me it was driving him crazy. Mostly he told me it was not easy.

He was surprised, for example, to discover how much time, patience, and energy it takes to get them dressed, fed, and out the door. I can remember the mornings when he was taking our two children to school:

"Can't you get them dressed before you leave?" My husband, attired in bathrobe and shaving cream, was close to pleading. I was dressed and ready to walk out the door. The fact that our daughter was still asleep appeared not to bother him at all.

Daddy's car soon became littered with the wrappings from whatever goodies he employed as the morning bribe to get the children out of the house; the back seat was filled with whatever stuffed animals our daughter decided she had to take with her.

My husband would describe it all in tones of wonder, much the way a tourist would describe his impressions of an exotic location.

"We get to her school," he would explain. "I get everyone out of the car and start walking to her classroom. Halfway there I turn around and discover nobody is following me. One is inspecting a piece of garbage on the ground and the other has wandered across to the playground." Once inside her school, the main attraction then for our two-year-old daughter was a bouncing horse. If she had logged mileage on the plastic beast, she would have ridden from New York to Washington.

"We get there some mornings," my husband would recount, "and she's already a little cranky. Then it turns out somebody else is riding the damn horse. You're talking major crisis. I'm ready to negotiate: 'Five bucks, kid, if you'll give my daughter her turn right away.' "

When we graduated to three children, once again I out-argued my husband into doing his fair share. For several (long) months, he took all three in the mornings. He thought he was a hero. By his own account, he must have been the only father in America to handle the morning shift. I would eavesdrop on his telephone conversations, and I could tell how desperate he was for a round of applause:

"I'll talk to you tomorrow," he would tell a business acquaintance over the phone. "No, I won't be in that early. I have to take the kids in the morning." (Pause for dramatic emphasis.) "All three of them."

A few days later he boasted: "I told this guy I was getting the kids ready in the mornings, and he was amazed. He told me not to tell his wife or she might get ideas." My husband smiled. I smiled. I'm sure the little woman would not have. My female friends, after all, saw nothing unusual or momentous in the fact that my husband was doing his share to take care of our children. Isn't that what liberated parenting is all about? Some of the preschool teachers, however, thought my husband was pretty adorable every morning. "He's so cute," they would say to me—leaving me to wonder: What did the other fathers do? Throw their children inside from a moving car? No teacher ever has told me I look cute arriving in the mornings.

Now I admit, getting three children fed, dressed, and out the door each day is a yeoman's job. It's like moving a flock: You continually round them up and nudge them forward. The odds on getting out of the house even remotely on time are about the same as winning the lottery. The job even involves remembering to take the lunchboxes and bottles I fixed the night before.

Which brings up a major point: I do try to help. I am not heartless or mean. Because my husband's brain is paralyzed in the mornings, I've tried to make his job easier. (We are dealing with a man who will step over a pile of clothes on the bottom stair and never even think of carrying them upstairs with him.) So I always have laid out the clothes and packed the lunches. I have written morning checklists and posted them everywhere from the refrigerator to the steering wheel of his car. I would dress any child who was ambulatory before I left the house. And yet, with my car keys in hand, numerous times I have heard him say: "Go on downstairs and Mom will give you breakfast."

Fathers, of necessity, can be mothers to invention. Working the morning shift prompted my husband to offer several revolutionary time-saving suggestions:

Skip baths every other night and wash only those portions of the body not covered by clothes. Likewise, let the kids wear the same clothes two days in a row if they are reasonably clean. Frequent washing wears out the fabric, my husband argues. (Love and laundry both start with "L," he quips, and they both go on forever.) Finally, he triumphantly urged, you can dress the children the night before. If they sleep in their clothes, they automatically are ready in the mornings.

Even with my help, however, the mornings can be tough for a man to handle. I have seen my husband's nerves start to unravel faster than a frayed rope.

I would ask my son: "Want me to get you dressed before I leave?"

"No," he would say. "Not yet."

My husband would whirl around. "Let Mom get you dressed," he would shout. "Please! Do it for me!"

Who could resist? "Daddy is upset," I would explain.

If the mornings are so difficult, you might wonder why my husband agreed to take them on instead of the evenings. Well, I wanted to work early so I could get home early. The schedule was best for the kids because it cut down on the number of hours they were away from home. My husband is more suited for working late because he always comes home late. In other words, while I am sure my husband will leave the house for the office every morning, I am never sure when (or if) he will leave the office to come home at night.

Anyway, I always have believed holding down the mornings is no worse than presiding over the nights. Mornings frayed him; nights tie me in knots. You want to talk pressure? The baby screams for his dinner; the other two are screaming for theirs. I already have cleaned up the kitchen from breakfast, cleaned out the lunch boxes from lunch, started dinner, given baths, and now I am slapping food on the plates as fast as I can. Talk about fast food.

"The applesauce isn't on the table," my son whines.

"Just wait! It's coming," I snarl.

My husband, who at that moment comes home, gets the applesauce. "Mommy is upset," he tells our son, the picture of calmness.

We have, twice in recent memory, switched assignments. He went to the office at dawn, while I took the kids to school and worked late. He picked them up.

The first time we switched, we only had two kids. When I

came home, an hour past dinnertime, the scene was pure chaos. My husband was the only one eating the leftovers I had designated for dinner. He had not washed out the lunchboxes or even brought in the afternoon mail. One child was screaming that he wanted to watch television; the other was just plain screaming. And deposited on the bathroom carpet was a heap of soaked underwear, socks, and shoes from somebody who hadn't quite gotten there in time. The look on my husband's face was something I hadn't seen since the first time I asked him to change a full diaper. I know the look on my face spoke volumes.

"These kids are impossible in the afternoons," he snarled. "They haven't stopped fighting since I picked them up. And don't criticize me."

Hey, I haven't. Until now.

The second time I had to be gone during the Suicide Hour, I fixed most of the dinner ahead. (What husband would do that for his wife?) But when I came home, it remained uneaten.

"What happened?" I asked. "What did you all eat?"

"We went out," my husband sheepishly explained. "I panicked."

Now that my office is my home, conscience prevents me from torturing my husband in the same squeeze play. Sure, he said he would continue to help with the mornings. "Tell me what you want me to do," he said. "Just because you don't have to go to the office doesn't mean I won't do my share." I suspect I've been conned, however. He appears to have suffered a bout of selective memory loss. He has forgotten how to feed or clothe a child in the morning. When he leaves for work, he doesn't make much of saying good-bye. Rather, he just slips out the back. One day, when he was complaining about how a sick child had ruined his sleep, he revealed his true feelings. "I know you're tired, too," he said. "But you can always take a nap during the day." For that remark, I shot him a look that could kill.

IN general, when it comes to forcing my husband to do his share, to experience the full brunt of parenting, I am ruthless. But even I have to admit, signing him up for a week's vacation alone with his children hit a new low.

Twice, because I could not take my vacation when his office was closed, I arranged matters so he soloed with the children. I rather enjoyed my respite from lunch boxes. My husband could not decide whether he was on vacation from work, or working on his vacation.

I can still see him, standing in the driveway—wearing his bathrobe and a three-day growth of beard—waving good-by. He looked only slightly more appealing than the garbage he had just taken out. I drove away wearing my dress-for-success skirt, sweater, pearls—and a big smile of relief. I knew my day was going to be easier than his. I was going to work; he was staying home with three children.

My husband did not appreciate the reality of this until the night before the vacation began. He was listing the chores he hoped to accomplish during his week off, when I reminded him two of our children would be home all day because the preschool was closed.

"Of course, you might as well keep the baby home, too," I added.

"Wait a minute," he protested. "How am I going to get anything done taking care of three kids?" I flashed him a women-do-it-every-day-smile and held my tongue.

My husband—I must give credit—had improved since he served a similar stint a year earlier and left the two year old in the same diaper all day. This second time he took reasonably good care of the kids; he was just not able to take care of anything else.

"It's impossible to do anything," he complained. "Somebody always needs to be changed, fed, dressed, or put to sleep. I can't do anything; we can't go anywhere. I need a reservation to take a shower." I declined to respond to his raised consciousness. I was already familiar with the frustration of erecting a high rise of plans on a foundation of sand.

If I suffered during his reign at home, I believed it was prudent to suffer in silence. Suffice it to say my husband's management style differs dramatically from my own. While I strive to project an image of total household control, his is one of chaos. He serves lunch any time between breakfast and dinner; it apparently varies in respect to begging. A careful excavation of the dishes piled in the sink each night reveals what the children finally ate, and in what order. Likewise, with naps my husband subscribes to the play-till-they-lay theory. He believes if a child is tired enough, he will sleep anywhere at any time.

I shuddered to phone home during the day. Somehow the screams and shrieks sound worse by telephone than in person. I coped badly hearing my husband's audio portion without the visual as he shouted: "Now you're in big trouble. I told you never, ever, to do that." Or, "Catch him, quick!"

When my husband is in charge he says he suspends the constitution and declares martial law. To me it feels more like anarchy. When I came home I found the kids dripping frozen fruit bars on the carpet while they watched television. My daughter had dressed herself in her party dress, and my son wore only a summer T-shirt under his winter jacket.

Don't misunderstand; I'm not complaining. It was wonderful to leave work each night not because the children were waiting, but because my work was done. And coming home was an adventure. It was like walking in on a play during the second act. You don't know what has happened already, so you don't know how things are supposed to turn out. Some nights I found every kid in the neighborhood assembled on my front lawn; other nights I found two sulky children confined to their beds. I never found dinner waiting on the table.

I did, however, find I had to readjust my sights. I had expected to breeze out the front door each morning and arrive early at work. Instead, I was late nearly every day that week. It takes a long time to hand out instructions.

But even when in my estimation my husband falls down, our children never notice Daddy has stumbled. They are not concerned with details. They do not care who folds the laundry, so long as it's in their drawers when they want it. They do not care who takes them to the doctor, so long as they get the medicine they need. And they are not angry with Daddy for working late; they are excited when they see him.

Maybe my children are smarter than their mother. They love Daddy for what he does, not despite what he does not. The scales probably balance. The times a man falls down as a husband, he frequently excels as a father. And vice-versa. It's just that I feel a bit like the little girl wearing a fancy dress who came to our door on Halloween. When I asked her what she was, she seemed to have trouble deciding. Finally, she said she was a princess-bride. Like that girl, I don't want to have to choose; I want to have it all.

11   The Daily Grind: My Life as a Coffee Bean

WE have approximately 20 minutes before it is time to leave the house for my work and her child care, but my daughter wastes ten of them refusing to get out of bed. In whispered tones, trying not to wake her sleeping brother, I cajole her out of her crib. Halfway through getting her dressed, she stages a sit-down strike and starts screaming. Downstairs, she is too angry to eat breakfast despite the eight minutes remaining for her to inhale sufficient calories to carry her through until her morning snack.

Eventually, now seven minutes late, I resort to violence and manhandle her out of the house and into the car. With the remorse born of hindsight, I recall shoving her into her car seat with more force than necessary. Her awakened brother, never slow to recognize an opportunity to score points, gives me an unusually sweet kiss and long hug before I head out the door. During this, I am annoyed to find myself glancing at my watch over his shoulder.

The louder my daughter screams as I try to get to work, the worse my driving becomes. I realize I am rattled when halfway to her school I have to return home because I have forgotten to take her lunch. Eventually she calms down in the car—

enough to nibble some toast—and I try to negotiate with utmost patience the treaty required every morning before she will vacate the car. Terms include where we should deposit her doll and toy rabbit before leaving them for the morning, and whether I am allowed to carry her lunchbox. Inside, I linger a few minutes before saying good-bye to make sure we are still on speaking terms. Headed to work, my late start means everyone else had a head start getting on the freeway, so the slow traffic makes me even later.

The subject is daily stress. To put it simply, working outside the home and having children is stressful. I compare it to a house of cards: everything is fine unless you run into a strong wind. One ear infection, or two spouses with two early morning meetings on the same day can be enough to send the entire structure tumbling. I would pull out of the driveway worrying about the baby's cough, and I would pull into the parking lot thinking about work. I would leave work planning the next day, and by the time I got home I would remember my son had no clean pajamas. Stress is a by-product of children compounded by obligations, such as the one to be at a certain place at a certain time. Getting to work becomes a hassle, matched only by getting home.

Contrary to all expectations, sometimes the hard part of my day has not been getting out the door, but picking up the children at school in order to come back home. For a while, when my son was five, my daughter was three, and my youngest was one, I worked full-time. Here is how evenings would go:

Arriving to pick up my children, I find my son in detention in the director's office. There he sits, hands folded neatly on his knees, sentenced to wait until his mother arrives. Already, I think to myself, a five-year-old delinquent. Would an expulsion go on his permanent record? Expecting the worst, I inquire: "What was his crime?"

He poked another child with his pencil.

"Tell your mother why you did that," his teacher instructs.

"Because he poked me," my son mutters.

"No, he didn't," the teacher says. "We've already talked about that. You poked him. Tell your mother why."

He can't. Rendered speechless through a combination of anger and mortification, he chooses instead to attempt to fold his face into my skirt. Finally, he pushes out the words: "I wanna tell you later, at home." Wordlessly he beseeches me. The director looks at me. We are suspended in silence. I realize I am unprepared to hold Significant Conversation; at the same instant I realize I am supposed to act parental and say something.

"Well, you need to promise your teacher never to do that again," I instruct as sternly as I can manage. "Then we'll talk about this at home." (We do, but I never get a straight answer.) The teacher releases us—and it's hard to say who feels more relieved.

I know it is possible to simply pick children up at school and leave. I've seen other parents do it. They would stride past me while I still hadn't negotiated past the doorway. I could not even walk; I had to tiptoe through an emotional minefield. If I arrived five minutes too late, for example, my children already would have started art. Then I would have to wait endlessly while they glued legs on paper dogs, strung beads, or got the eyeholes cut in their paper masks. If it wasn't art, then we would have to wait for the end of a story.

Sometimes when I came to school I would see my son's face glower at me through the window. Then I would know somebody had told him his mother was there.

"Don't tell me!" he would shout. "I already know!" But of course everybody rushed to tell him. And, of course, the more they did the angrier he got.

Once we established basic agreement that we were going to leave, then would come packing up. Each morning they took their lunch boxes and jackets. Each evening they would bring home at least five different papers apiece including drawings, music sheets, newsletters, and art projects—all requiring individual admiration. We would discuss technique to properly appreciate how the macaroni came to be glued to the paper. We had to remember to retrieve the lunch boxes and jackets. And, on bad days, my daughter also brought her wet pants home in a plastic bag. Of course they handed it all to me to balance in my hands along with the baby and the car keys.

Once we reached the car, the battle began over seating arrangements. For a long time the baby had the honor of sitting next to Mommy. When he moved to the back, the battle switched to who got to sit next to baby. Then, after that novelty wore off, the battle switched to who got to be in front. To end the fighting, I decided that whoever sat in back had the right to pick the cassette we would play. Big mistake. That worked once—then they began to argue over who got to sit in back.

Even those days we have had an entire afternoon to decompress, I found afternoons could be stressful. When my daughter was two and my son was four, I worked half days. But even my afternoons never seemed to go the way I envisioned.

I would pick up my daughter just as she awakened from her nap. Theoretically she was refreshed, but in reality she was groggy and cranky. She cried because I took her sweater off and screamed when I tried to put it back on. We would make slow progress to the car, and during the drive home I would remember the unwashed breakfast dishes awaiting me.

Coaxing the toddler into her high chair, I would elect to let her decorate herself with yogurt in order to gain time while I attacked the kitchen and prepared another in my repertoire of dinners that can be made ahead and later left unattended in the oven. On the days she finished before I did, we would not have a salad that evening.

Then we'd head upstairs where she got a new diaper, I would slip into non–dry-clean-only clothes, and then start the struggle to get her downstairs to the car to pick up her brother. This would take a bit of time because every activity would be punctuated by her current battle cry: "I do it!" Foolishly, I would attempt to hold her hand on the stairway. She would set me straight by screaming and then climbing back up to the top to do it again by herself. When we got her brother, the coaxing process would start in reverse because she always decided his school was more interesting than our car. Eventually, we would arrive home where I frequently managed to place my purse in a puddle on the kitchen counter.

My son would beg to watch television, but in my mind we were scheduled for "quality time," so we would compromise with a walk outside. This would yield such excitement as watching workmen pour a new sidewalk, a visit with a dog who licked my daughter's hands before I could stop him, and a few futile minutes trying to convince the kids we could all play ball together without fighting.

Inside, we would reread the latest library book (I promised myself never to check out anything that long again) and I would begin waging a propaganda campaign to get them both into the bathtub. Once there, my son would refuse to vacate until Daddy came home for dinner. Hence, when said husband would slink in the door 45 minutes late, he would be greeted by one puckered son and a dried-out meatloaf. My daughter, who would realize at that instant she was starving, would begin screaming inconsolably for me to hold her at the precise moment I was trying to put dinner on the table. She would grip my kneecaps with surprising strength. Eventually, we would all sit down and eat—together, just like a family on television.

Stress, however, shows no favorites. It visits even on the days I stay home. For six months after my youngest was born, I stayed home full time. It was not exactly a picnic.

When my husband comes home from work at 6 P.M., I am exactly where he first saw me at 6 a.m. He kisses me goodbye in the morning while I am still groggy from the 4 A.M. feeding. I am changing the baby's wet diaper, trying to talk the toddler out of hers, and arguing with the four year old about getting dressed.

"How is this tie with this jacket?" he wants to know, adding his voice to the clamor before walking out the door. And, since I am home, would I please take some suits to the cleaners?

Two hours later—the house in some semblance of order and each child having eaten twice—we leave. Walking out, I realize I am wearing my jeans and their stain on the left leg for the third straight day. We circle the parking lot at the cleaners until we get a space by the curb. Then I pile the cleaning into a basket from the nearby grocery store. Juggling the baby on my shoulder, I shepherd the other two onto the sidewalk with one holding onto my purse and the other the basket. At the sidewalk, my son immediately disappears into the nearby bakery.

Two (small) cookies later, we head to the YMCA to register the two year old for a tumbling class. This venture degenerates into a battle. They both want something from the lobby vending machine. As I am explaining why mommies don't approve of candy and chips, another mother gives her son a quarter to buy a candy bar. Then, in the parking lot, the baby wants to eat.

At home I push the stroller while the other two ride bikes

around the block. We are halfway home when my daughter refuses to ride any more. Pushing the stroller and carrying her tricycle, I find it impossible to walk without bruising the back of my legs.

Lunchtime. My (starving) daughter cries for her milk and sandwich; my son demands juice. The new bottle of juice is in the back of the bottom cabinet in front of which I have parked the baby sleeping in his stroller. After I dig it out, I cannot open the bottle, but in the process I do wake up the baby. He wants to eat.

I set up the children painting water colors so I can settle the baby to nurse. The two year old cries because the four year old tells her his picture is better. She takes two swipes with her brush and announces she is done. The baby is not.

Naptime. Two are down to sleep and I seize the chance to catch up on chores. The phone rings. A cousin wants to know if I've gotten anyone to come in to help me. "Well then," she advises, "at least you should rest when the baby is asleep." While I am on the phone, the four year old uses his doctor kit to give the sleeping baby an examination. "It's OK, Mom," he announces. "The baby is alive."

The noise from my neighbor's lawn mower awakens my daughter early. For the next half hour she cries in response to any attempts at communication. The baby, who wants to eat, also cries. We manage to spend the rest of the afternoon outside where my daughter spills an entire bottle of bubbles and my son digs in great quantities of dirt.

Dinnertime. I strip my son of his mud-covered clothes, and belatedly realize my daughter has not been changed since before her nap. Thus, when my husband walks in, I am changing the baby's diaper, trying to talk the toddler into changing hers, and trying to talk my son into putting on some clothes.

"Hi," he smiles. "How was your day?" As I formulate a reply—the baby wants to eat.

UNTIL I found myself avidly devouring an article about new ideas for lunchbox cuisine, I never realized how close to the edge my kids have pushed me. I do not yet shape my meatloaves into snowmen or my pancakes into Mickey Mouse ears, but I have begun reading ingredient labels and trying to balance my previously lopsided meals. Likewise, I never used to care what designs were on diapers, but now I know that to my children Sesame Street is a designer label.

I have come so far, because for me feeding and diapering have replaced recreational sports. They are mundane chores, but they stretch on forever. If you think paying the utility bills every month is irritating, try feeding a five month old every three hours or potty training a three year old. It's like making the beds every morning to the power of five. You know they will only get messed up again, but you have to do it anyway. It's like picking up one room only to find that—like a swarm of locusts—the kids have moved their destruction to another. For a mother it's an exercise in futility called running in place.

Feeding comes first, and no wonder. Babies undergo more weigh-ins than a prizefighter, and no mother wants to fall behind when it comes to growth-chart competition. A good mother has sassy babies who rank high above the fiftieth percentile; a failure does not. So stuffing babies with milk easily occupies much of an infant's waking hours and much of a mother's time. You will know your baby is sufficiently full when you can hear whitecaps swishing in his stomach.

Some babies eat so slowly they seem to start one meal

minutes after finishing the last. The introduction of rice cereal doesn't improve the situation—it only doubles the feeding time. After a baby's initial astonishment at solid food, the trick becomes guaranteeing that enough glides down his throat to ensure proper nourishment. (This persists until the preteen years when the problem becomes locking them out of the refrigerator.) Mothers must perfect the art of shoving a spoon into the back of a baby's throat—just short of gagging range but far enough to ensure swallowing. (Quell your conscience. If you think strained green beans look bad remember you are dealing with a discerning infant who also will stuff his mouth with toilet paper, sand, and dirt.) The process can take hours; breakfast is barely consumed before it is time for lunch.

A child's mealtime adds whole new meanings to the words "mess" and "laundry." Somehow, the infant barely capable of standing, manages to coordinate hand and eye sufficiently to deflect the spoon of food heading toward his mouth. My children also effectively have used their tongues to snowplow out of their mouths any food they did not want. Then there's the first time your child feeds himself with a spoon. Until your baby has an itch or a sneeze, you cannot understood how a child can get cereal in his ear, peas in his eyebrows, and pears up his nose. A toddler's entire menu is revealed, daily, in the stains on the front of the clothes you thought were covered completely by a bib. Your child is getting older when at last he manages to eat as much as he spills. When he is full, then no matter how much is left, he is likely to spill it all. My toddlers have always concluded their meals by dropping food bombs off their high chairs to splat upon the floor below.

Once the basic skills are established, then briefly follows the golden age of eating. A toddler, too young to be prey to prejudices, is always hungry and will sample almost anything. At times my son would tell me what he ate for lunch at preschool, and then we would decide what he was going to eat for lunch at home. Enjoy the few brief months of earnest eating, because then comes the onset of the picky eater. At this stage, recall the words of that astute pediatrician who said he never yet saw a child starve himself to death. You will wonder, nevertheless, if it is possible for a child to overdose on crackers. During this time, meals can be defined as anything eaten between snacks.

You will learn the rules of food according to your youngster. You will learn to take orders regarding the color of the juice cup or into which compartment of the plate the food is to be deposited. (Woe to the mother who lets the vegetables touch the meat.) You will learn to ask permission before cutting the food or breaking the cracker. (Many a graham cracker has been rejected because it was served "small.") You will put up with a child who refuses to eat anything yellow. You will learn to mask your true feelings from a child who eats only American cheese because Swiss is "for mice," or a child who refuses any fruit he classifies as "squishy." You will remain impassive before a child who refuses to eat fresh, sweet garden peas, but gobbles down the bright green substitutes from the freezer. And, above all, you will try to pretend it really doesn't matter to you whether a child eats or not. This attitude is essential for credibility when you tell your child: "I don't care if you eat dinner, but just remember you won't get anything else before bedtime."

Finally, when you notice yourself buying bigger quantities at the grocery store, or when an audience gathers to watch you pack lunches, you will know your child's stomach is headed toward maturity. Then you will join millions of mothers singing in chorus: "Nothing but fruit before dinner." You will learn to hold dessert hostage as reward for a good meal. And on occasion, you will learn to give in. For you also will know that food is important not only because it provides nourishment. You also will know that a child busy stuffing his mouth can neither complain nor scream.

A child who stuffs his mouth, of course, also does something else. To put it another way, what goes in must come out. Which brings up another preoccupation for new parents: diapers and everything that goes with them. From their appearance to their regularity, never before have you attached so much importance to bowel movements.

Now, if your good china isn't plastic and your lawn furniture isn't made by Little Tikes, then you may have trouble imagining how this can happen. When we furnished the nursery, I did not realize our babies would spend nearly as much time on the changing table as in the crib. The diaper companies say the average baby has his diaper changed 2,000 times during his first six months. That's the opposite of an exaggeration, if your child, like mine, usually does his business right after you put him in a fresh diaper. (The average second baby, however, probably has his diaper changed somewhat less.)

Understandably, prevalent wisdom advises against having two children in diapers at once. Since I was never good at taking advice (or planning ahead), that is precisely what happened to me. Nothing like changing a newborn to make you realize what a giant your older child has become. This is usually the time parents forsake the changing table for the bed, and start the big push toward potty training. Now diapers do not disgust me, not even what is in them. But when a child turns two, visions of diaperless freedom begin to dance in my head. Since potty training is an entrance requirement for preschool, usually I feel some urgency about the matter. After five unrelenting years of use, the diaper pail has carved a permanent divot into my carpet. I would gladly forfeit my brand loyalty;

it only extends as far as which diaper company is offering a coupon, anyway.

But my eagerness is tempered by experience. Potty training should be included in Dante's vision of hell. I can remember my husband shouting excitedly that our daughter, then twenty months, wanted to use the potty. He hauled her upstairs to the bathroom, stripped her, and waited. I didn't bother to hang around. His enthusiasm wasn't catching. She wanted to copy everything that her big brother did, but that didn't mean she could. Potty training is awash with false hopes. I could plop her little fanny onto the potty seat at her insistence, all right, but once she got there my daughter hadn't a clue what was to transpire.

I have learned that potty training, like heaven, can wait. I would rather be condemned to six consecutive hours listening to Wee Sing cassettes. Parents begin potty training at the distinct disadvantage that occurs any time children have something that their parents want—in this case, control over their own bladders. To embark upon the months-long ordeal of potty training, a parent must be prepared to curb his temper and load the washing machine. A child who wets his pants five times a day isn't necessarily trying to be bad, and the saleslady who told you six pairs of training pants would be enough wasn't necessarily trying to mislead you.

It is difficult, I will grant you, not to scream at a child who denies any need to potty two minutes before flooding the floor. Positive strategies, the books say, are called for. Some parents periodically sit a child on the potty, surrounded by ample reading material or favorite toys, and keep him there until nature takes its course. Then they declare victory and end the siege. Eventually, however, a child must become a participant and go to the potty when he knows he has to. He has to be taught to heed nature's signal. In my son's case, he not only heeded it, but he must have anticipated it. You see, I resorted to bribery: A cookie for every successful trip. Some hours he polished off three or four cookies. Other known bribes include using colorful targets that float in the toilet bowl and change color after a direct hit, or the promise of wearing highly coveted underwear adorned with favorite cartoon characters.

Once you start, of course, come those awkward times when a child is only partially trained and the effort seems only partially worth it. You will know you have entered this twilight zone when you line the car seat with towels before taking a diaper-less child on a substantial auto trip, or when the trainee wakes you in the middle of the night to announce he wet the bed. Before I lock the front door now and go anywhere, automatically I order all ambulatory children into the bathroom.

Along with potty training comes a host of fun-filled related issues such as hand washing and modesty. In hyping hygiene, I admit to portraying the onslaught of germs as something akin to the invasion of Normandy. I have resigned myself that my bathroom countertops never again will be free of puddles. On the matter of modesty, the best I can say is that both children are always fully dressed by the time they leave the house.

Potty training is a time of inconvenience. It marks the demise of coveralls and rompers and all the other darling outfits your child could not possibly remove himself to go to the bathroom. It also means you must learn the location of the bathroom in every public place you visit, because you will spend a lot of time loitering in front of it. The one time at the library I didn't loiter, I was paged after the librarian heard my son calling for help through the door. Yes, I have seen the inside of more men's rooms than in my entire previous life. Yes, I even have abandoned the grocery checkout line with my basket half unloaded.

In the end, if you insist on going through with the training, peer pressure is more effective than parental pressure. Most children cannot long endure the telltale shame of soggy disgrace before their colleagues. You will know you have completed your child's initiation to maturity when he no longer comes home from school bearing his clothes in a plastic bag, and no longer insists on saving his "accomplishments" for Daddy to admire.

So while I know successful potty training promises nirvana, I also know first comes purgatory. For an endless while I used to moan that my son was "perfectly" potty trained: He only had accidents when we had company, when we were on the way out the door, when he was in bed, or when he had no clean clothes left. Twice I picked him up from preschool to find him wearing his pants backward with no underwear. So even though I know potty training is a necessary rite of passage, I am in no hurry to pass that way again. I have one child left, and by the time he is ready for kindergarten I'm sure he will have taken care of it by himself.

IN my household, "regularity" is not just a word that applies to the potty. As regularly as there are mouths to feed and diapers to change, there is medicine to administer.

As I write these words, in fact, I have a cold. My nose is tender, my throat is raw, my ears ring, and my head feels the way a cotton ball looks.

This is no ordinary cold. I know its complete pedigree. My daughter caught it from her girlfriend down the street, my toddler caught it from his sister, and I caught it from my son. I wish I could say we didn't always share this much, but we do. When I first had children I expected they would bring a lot of changes to my life—but never did I expect they would usher in so much disease. Before I became a mother, I had never been so sick.

We are talking nothing dramatic here. No typhus, scarlet fever, or measles. I would consider those all-out frontal assaults on my well being. No, we are talking sniper attacks. An insidious guerrilla warfare that day after day simply grinds me down with the same ailments over and over again.

Lots of things about rearing children are difficult. There is colic, there is teething, there is temper, and there is potty training. Eventually there is even dating and driving. But they pale in comparison to illness. Disease and pestilence have filled my medicine cabinets, emptied my wallet, and helped me accumulate an amazing assortment of medicine droppers, measuring spoons, and cups. Faster than the insurance company can reimburse me for one claim, I have filed three more. No week in recent memory has my entire family been free of colds, coughs, flu, or ear infections. I've been through impetigo, earaches, asthma, allergies, and even a skin rash that disappeared every time I asked the doctor to take a look.

In my family we fall like dominoes, one after the other. Sometimes I think even the germs must be complaining about the congestion. In one week my baby has suffered from stomach flu, a cold, and teething. I have taken the same child to the same doctor twice in the same week for two different ailments. My idea of a perfect invention would be a button, like a turkey thermometer, that pops out of the baby to signify an ear infection.

Not surprisingly, I have come to know the pediatrician and the pediatrician's office well. Headwaiters don't greet me by name. Neither do the checkers at my regular grocery store. But at the pediatrician's office, the receptionist not only knows my name but spells it correctly. While I would prefer to believe she remembers us because my children are so charming, I rather fear it's because my children are sick so often.

When I was pregnant, I interviewed potential pediatricians. That was before I knew childhood is to disease as a sweater is to lint: One attracts the other. So I queried doctors on their philosophies and inspected their credentials. I looked for warm smiles and organized waiting rooms. Never did I think to ask if the doctor would be in on Saturday nights, if he would throw in some medicine for me while dosing my child, or if he offered a discount for seeing two kids on one visit. Now I'm ready for a line of revolving credit. Now I know that to qualify for insurance coverage, it's best to schedule a wellness visit when the child is sick. And I'm not above trying to arrange for my child to cough loudly near the phone when I have the doctor on the line, so he can tell me if the congestion warrants a visit.

Of course, I wasn't always so pragmatic. At first I was awed. Pediatricians are imbued with god-like qualities to many first-time parents. I spent hours trying to interest my firstborn in his hands, because the pediatrician said he was supposed to become fascinated by finger movements. Was he behind because he only wanted to teethe on his toes?

Some pediatricians advise mothers on everything: how long to nurse, how long to let the baby sleep, what to do if he doesn't. Others advise practically nothing. As one mother lamented: "The doctor would say, 'See you in three months,' and I'd want to say, 'Wait—that's a long time. Don't you have anything else to tell me before then?'" I asked my doctor once if perhaps older parents were more capable of coping with medical mishaps. "No," he replied, giving me a sideways glance. "Older mothers seem to have more fertile imaginations."

Recently I saw a neighbor bringing her seven year old home

from his checkup. No more scheduled visits, she marveled, until he goes away to camp. Personally, I can't imagine a time when the only reason we would visit the doctor is because camp requires a checkup. I can't imagine a time when one of my kids doesn't scream hysterically at the sight of the doctor, or doesn't wait until after office hours to become seriously ill.

But even if some day his receptionist no longer recognizes us on sight, I guess we'll stay with the same old doctor. My kids know their way around the examining rooms and I know my way around the appointment book. We've invested a lot of time and energy into breaking the doctor in. He doesn't flinch when my son swings his stethoscope like a lasso, and he knows that my kids throw punches when he tries to examine their ears. The doctor's office is one of the few places in town where I feel the entire family is welcome. It wasn't my son, after all, who broke the fish tank in the waiting room.

Way back when my oldest was newborn—and before I knew we would become regulars—I remember asking the pediatrician about germs.

"After he drops the pacifier," I inquired, "should I sterilize it?"

"Nonsense," the doctor answered. "A baby needs to be exposed to germs. That's the only way he can build up resistance." I have taken his words to heart. I keep telling myself we are doing our suffering in advance. By kindergarten my children will have contracted every virus known to man and they won't get sick at all. But somehow I don't believe it. There will always be new virus strains, resistant to all but the most expensive antibiotics, to plague us until adolescence. There will always be new inopportune times for illness to strike. The baby chose to begin vomiting, for example, on the way to the airport to pick up Grandma in rush-hour traffic the night before

Thanksgiving. It's sort of like soaring to new heights of aggravation as you sink to new depths of misery.

In my family, medicine has become a status symbol. This is partly because children's medicine is flavored to taste like the candy my children ordinarily are denied, and partly because whoever remains healthy starts to feel left out. My daughter once complained that she doesn't also get allergy shots. I admit succumbing, occasionally, to their peer pressure. I have dispensed half a dropper of pain reliever in the absence of true pain, just as I have applied unnecessary bandages to microscopic owies.

Because in my family it is chic to be sick, diagnoses are difficult.

"I don't want this," my daughter says, pushing away her plate. "He's not eating," she says, pointing to her genuinely-ailing brother.

"Well, he shouldn't eat," I reply. "He's sick."

"So am I," she responds.

"What's the matter? Where does it hurt?"

"I'm sick," she says, "in my elbow."

12 Great Expectations and Low Hopes

PERIODICALLY all mothers go a little soft in the brain at the notion of planning special family events. I envision these events through a camera whose lens blurs the rough edges of reality, like the misty image on a greeting card. In my mind's eye I imagine a special outing at the museum, ball game, or concert at which a beatific child tightly clasps my hand—enraptured by a joyful experience— and showers me with smiles of love.

In focusing on this picture, I shun logic, past experience, and the laws of rational behavior. All too often the vision is as much like the true picture as the post card is like the vacation— and the beatific child is really a brat. In terms of expectations, it's like presenting your child with a special gift, and then realizing he enjoys the box it came in more than the toy itself.

To a parent, childhood is composed of a million special moments—most of them unplanned. As a mother I am continually surprised when things I had expected to be wonderful, turn out to be less than that. Children are as likely to remember a visit to the park as they are an expensive vacation. Events highly anticipated can turn into emotional donnybrooks of disappointment.

As a new mother I didn't know the rule of misplaced expectations. When my oldest child was only two, my friend had to explain to me some of these hard facts of life. The mother of three, she saved me from myself. I had proposed taking our children together to see a play. With a series of deft observations, she brought me to my senses: "That's a 45 minute drive in rush hour traffic," she said. "The show is right at naptime when the kids are getting cranky. It lasts over an hour; they'll never sit still that long." And the topper: "They'll both have to potty and we'll be sitting nowhere near the aisle." We never went.

My friend is no spoilsport, just smart. Excursions undertaken with good intentions can turn into bad times. First of all, it is not easy to go anywhere with small children. A baby requires so much equipment that the diaper bag has to be packed like a suitcase, and the car feels like a moving van. Not only do you have to haul the bag with you, but upon arrival someone has to lug it—as well as the tired child.

The time for going anywhere is limited. You must plan to be there between naps, before the next trip to the potty, and in time for the next feeding. Juggling the schedules of two or more kids, this can leave you about 20 available minutes per day. We have driven 20 minutes to a special children's restaurant for dinner, only to find three kids asleep in the car upon arrival. Maybe some children wake up cheerfully; they aren't mine. We have planned to spend the day at a special hands-on children's museum, only to find that the two year old was out of sorts and threw a screaming fit when he had to wait his turn at an exhibit. We have spent a small fortune on parking and admission to an amusement park only to find that the lines in front of the rides stretched longer than a child's patience. And while the price of admission certainly may be worth an entire day's entertainment, we've never had the kind of children who can last the entire day.

I never gave up on the idea of taking my children to a play, however. I want my children to know television is not the highest art form. So after waiting three years, my husband and I finally took *three* children to the theater instead of one. I should have listened to my own advice.

I suspected we were in trouble driving in the car when my daughter, then two, couldn't grasp the concept of a play. "It's something you see," I explained, "not something you do." I knew we were in trouble when outside the theater I saw the souvenir hucksters. While the show was pretty good child's fare, my son's loud and incessant demands for a toy just about ruined it.

After intermission I noticed the woman next to me returned to her seat with popcorn in the bathtub size and two flashlights with crystals that glow in the dark. She confirmed our opposition to buying souvenirs when she had to take them both away after one boy hit his brother, and the other broke his light trying to hit back. Like a lot of parents, she was among those who left early. We left late—but not late enough to avoid the tenacious souvenir sellers and the gridlock in the parking lot. Imagine more than 500 cars, each filled with tired, overstimulated children needing to potty, and all trying to exit at the same time. Now imagine how the parents were driving.

That night I waited for my children to express their delight and gratitude. Nothing came, so I primed the pump with questions: "How did you like it? Did you enjoy a real, live play?" My daughter told me with excitement that she loved it. "It was," she said, "a great movie."

For these reasons among others, I have become an habitue of the neighborhood park. Close and convenient, the park can rate as highly to a child as driving two hours to the zoo. But repeated visits have made me realize even the park never quite measures up to the fantasy I used to see in my mind's eye.

Never once have I sat sunning on the bench with a novel while my children played happily for hours.

There are two basic approaches to an outing at the park. The first is hit-and-run. It involves no packing, no equipment, and no expectations. You simply play for a little while and then haul everyone home. The second is the expedition. This involves making a day of it. In addition to sand toys, strollers, lunches, and bicycles, I also have seen mothers haul portable playpens and wind mobiles to the park. These same mothers spread out colorful blankets under the trees and chat for hours with their friends while their kids cavort.

I tend to be more of the hit-and-run variety. I draw the line at spending more time loading and unloading than in actual playing. And even when I come with friends, our children inevitably end up at opposite ends of the park and demand our separate, personal supervision. They rarely cavort. My daughter wants pushes on the swing, her son persists in standing at the top of the slide, and my son is fighting with a boy who "stole" his hole. I define optimism as a mother who brings along a novel but not extra diapers.

No matter how long you stay, of course, you're still faced with the basic problem of leaving. This involves both convincing the children to go, and then cleaning them up. When it is time to go, my children become very busy. They mix wet sand, for example, and then slop it all over the fish statue in the corner of the park. They are, so they say, giving the fish a bath. It is hard work and it totally absorbs their attention. Too bad they waited to start until I told them it was time to go home. The more I mention leaving, the more industrious they become. Depending on your schedule and mood, you either resort to bribery or to force. For a long time my children believed the road home from the park detoured through the frozen yogurt shop. But after the fourth time we have stayed for only "five more minutes," I have been known to bodily haul a reluctant child to the car.

Before you get in the car, you have to shake out your child. Do not take your children to the park on the day you aspire to skip their baths. Each week it comes as something of a surprise to me that the level of sand at the park does not appreciably diminish—surely most of it has come home in my children's shoes and cuffs. The day my daughter discovered the water fountain and the enormous possibilities of wet sand, she had to ride home in her underwear.

At my park there is an unwritten rule that toys left unattended may be "borrowed" until claimed by their owner. This is a boon to variety, but also offers the spectacle of two children fighting for possession of something neither of them owns. So much for my fantasy that my children will share. Toys also tend to disappear; so lately instead of buckets we have been digging with empty Cool Whip containers. (A personal note: Whoever ended up with our blue plastic rake, I wish you better luck. My children turned it into a lethal weapon.)

So why do I keep coming back to the same swingset every week? Because the children love it, because it's something that mothers do, because it fits the fantasy of great expectations, and because it's a place to meet other mothers in the same boat as you are. Even parents whose children cannot yet walk bring them to the park, eager to coax a smile by teaching them the joys of swinging.

Some parents come even sooner. One day, as we were leaving the park after some particularly vigorous protests, I saw a pregnant woman walking slowly by. She wore an understated career woman's maternity dress with pumps and matching purse. As she strolled around the perimeter of the park, she seemed rather wistful to me. She seemed to be dreaming of the day when she would become a mother and be initiated into the sorority at the park. She probably could hardly wait for her chance to push the swing, to stand guard duty at the slide, and to picnic cozily on a blanket. I didn't stop and talk to that woman. I let her enjoy her fantasy. Ignorance is bliss.

THANKSGIVING does not often find us going over the river and through the woods to grandmother's house. Instead— carrying three children up well past their bedtime, three suitcases, a car seat, and plastic baby doll—one year it found us battling airport holiday crowds to fly there. No inconvenience, I silently and repeatedly reminded myself as I waited for our delayed flight, warrants keeping the children apart from their relatives during a holiday.

I'm sure that as a child, I too was the focus of a lemming-like urge to gather for every occasion. But until I became a parent, I never realized how intense the holiday pressure can be. Now my husband and I dole out our presence like gold stars awarded to the side of the family whose turn it is to share the particular season with us. And as a mother, I find it impossible to let a holiday slip by without proper decorations and celebrations. The front door has been adorned with everything from Indian corn to Cupid to pictures of the presidents.

I used to scoff at some of the mothers I encountered. They hand-crafted decorations for the house and sewed identical Christmas outfits to be worn in the annual holiday portrait photographed ahead in September. Now, as a mother who spent weeks planning a birthday party for a mere four children, I can understand their frenzy every bit as much as I envy their organizational ability.

Children bring out the holiday in everyone. Not only birthdays, but the deluge between Halloween and Valentine's Day brings an overwhelming urge to make them picturebook family affairs. Well, now I know a thing or two about photo albums: You don't always know what you're looking at. I can remember at my wedding how the photographer monopolized me and my husband, driving us close to the edge. I can remember snarling at my husband that I wouldn't let the man take another shot. That photo, snapped as I snarled, is one of the best in the book. Everyone remarks about how happy I look.

For the record, let me state that special occasions do bring special moments. I have treasured my share of hand-lettered Valentines and swallowed a lump in my throat as my children paraded proudly for the Fourth of July to the strains of John Phillip Sousa blaring out of a neighbor's stereo. We have also had fun carving pumpkins and competing in the neighborhood costume contest. And airports aside, we always manage to make Thanksgiving a special family time.

But at other times, such as when I am signing my daughter's name to 36 store-bought Valentines almost identical to those she will receive, I wonder if it's necessary to work so hard at holidays. The more I anticipate, the harder I fall. Holidays sometimes seem better done by Hallmark.

We celebrate Chanukah in our house, and Chanukah, in this way, has always been the source of a letdown. In the beginning, I didn't want to make very much of it. Before the kids were old enough to catch the Christmas hype going on all around them, we didn't do much in the way of presents. But now I understand why a festival celebrating religious freedom has turned into a celebration centered around children and presents. Parents don't want their children to feel left out of any holiday season.

I can remember when I realized I was sounding just like other parents talking about naughty and nice. My son wouldn't come downstairs for breakfast because in my supreme stupidity

I had served the eggs without timing breakfast to a commercial. After that, his behavior degenerated from bad to worse. He picked a fight with his sister about who got to open the front door, he refused to get dressed, and then he wouldn't nap. I knew my parenting skills had run dry when I found myself admonishing, "Just because it's Chanukah time doesn't mean you are going to get any presents. We give those to boys and girls who behave—something you certainly haven't done to-day!"

Inwardly I groaned at the depths to which I had sunk. But the practical part of me recognizes that even bribery has its place—provided it works. In a few more years my son probably will recognize what I already know. Short of criminal indict-ment, he's going to get at least some presents no matter how he behaves.

But that's the point. Chanukah has turned into a holiday about presents: my running around trying to buy them and the children panting to receive them. Just as I was sounding like other parents, my children had been sounding like other kids with their unabashed greed. We give each child one pres-ent per night, a total harvest of eight during the course of the holiday. I believe keeping a cap on the number of presents builds fortitude and strength of character—like keeping the thermostat turned low in the winter.

My children, however, have shown little character. We pres-ent the presents after dinner. This provides an added benefit because the children finish their food, including vegetables, much more quickly when they know a surprise is waiting for them. On the first night, after opening his present, my son asked me where were the rest. I reminded him that we give one per night. He sprinted from the table to the guest bedroom to fish anxiously under the bed where the previous year I had hidden all the gifts. Nothing. He thrashed around the room.

Glumly he returned, casting me reproachful looks. The second
night my daughter knew what was coming. Before I even had
served the food she asked: "Presents tonight, Mommy?"

"Yes," I replied, speaking loudly so her brother also would
hear. "But the presents aren't important. It's the spirit of the
holiday. When we light the candles tonight, remember what
we are celebrating."

"Yes," she agreed, and even nodded. "But where are the
toys?"

By the sixth night, we were on a roll with behavior ap-
proaching something you might expect of anyone on a Twinkie
diet. "Is everyone done eating?" my son would bellow after
bolting his food and favoring me with anticipatory grins. He
actually glowered at his father for helping himself to second
servings.

But Chanukah is a festival of miracles, and I'm happy to
report one. Nothing like I had anticipated, but a nice turna-
round nevertheless. On the eighth and final night last year, we
gave no toys in my household. Eagerly my children tore the
wrappings from their presents only to find winter jackets. Mentally, I braced myself for recriminations. To my surprise, my
son smiled sweetly, gave me a big kiss, and sincerely thanked
me. And my daughter, well, she wanted to sleep in hers.

❧

I AM standing landlocked in the party goods aisle, paralyzed
before the bags of plastic snakes, performing mental arithmetic,
trying to divide the number of snakes into the price of the bag
and then to multiply that by the number of boys possibly
coming to my five year old's birthday party. There is nothing
like being heavy into goodie bags. I would have laughed at
myself, but it isn't funny. Birthday parties, whether you are

the giver or the parent of the attender, are serious business. What other event raises earth-shattering considerations such as how to award prizes after a game in such a way that no child actually is declared a winner?

Birthday parties generate a fever in children and a trepidation in parents. Like fraternity hazing, they can be an unavoidable and raucous rite of passage. Every child over the age of two demands a party, and every photo album includes pictures of blowing out the candles. But parties are stressful to the parents who give them, to the children who attend, and to the child they honor. Few have ever been idyllic.

The invitation to the first official party to which my son was ever invited came ten days before the event. This allowed him to build up a lather of anticipation and hysteria. My son's first response to the invitation brought up the issue most important to him: the present. He suggested that perhaps he could give his friend one of his old toys. My suggestion was that we go to the store to pick out something together. Big mistake. Whenever possible, buy the educational and inexpensive toy by yourself. Otherwise, reaching agreement with your child upon a suitable birthday present is no more complicated than peace talks to end any major war. You both assume non-negotiable positions.

When I buy a toy, I put myself in the other parent's shoes and ask myself these questions: How many pieces am I willing to pick up off the floor? How would I clean it up if it spilled? Could I stand something in my home that makes that kind of noise? And, exactly how much damage would be sustained by the child hit over the head with it? In addition, I rule out guns, any toy based upon a television show, and anything costing more than $10. My son's first choices were an authentic-looking submachine gun or a $90 telescope. We compromised with a modeling dough toy. You press the dough inside a monster head, turn the screw, and the dough comes sliming out through the eyes, mouth, and ears. The mother might not appreciate it, I decided, but the kid should love it. I wanted him to be happy; the birthday boy was a special buddy from preschool. Only the week before he and my son had been reprimanded together for digging a hole under the school fence. (Trying to tunnel out, they told the teacher.)

I learned a few things from observing that first birthday party. Try to hold them outside, where vacuuming is not an issue. This one was at the park so the mother wasn't upset when four kids spilled the bottles of soap bubbles they received in their goodie bags, or when somebody tipped the cake off the table just after the last piece was cut. At this party the boys came in play clothes and the girls came in pretty dresses; within ten minutes everyone was barefoot and filthy.

I learned that parents have to maintain control over the presents. The host, of course, has the right to greet each guest and grab the present. But I have seen parties where the guests proceeded to rip open them all. The only thing nobody bothered to tear open were the cards. Suffice it to say even under the best of circumstances the present opening does not resemble a genteel baby shower where smiling women pass each gift around and someone keeps track for thank-you notes. After a gift is opened, it is a mother's solemn duty to whisk it away and out of reach until the party is over, lest it be totally destroyed in minutes.

The other thing I learned is that ending a birthday party is as important as deciding to have it. I know one mother who did not put a pick-up time on her invitations. She ended up with twelve whiny girls at a party that lasted for eight hours. As another mother put it, the best part of giving her first birthday party was that all the kids were picked up on time.

Even having culled these bits of wisdom, I have never felt sufficiently fortified or prepared for giving my own parties.

When I was pregnant, I had long arms. I know this because I used to pat myself on the back for having three winter babies. No sweaty summer pregnancies for me. I didn't realize, of course, that winter parties have to be held inside—and I didn't anticipate how much damage a herd of five year olds can do to a living room. Likewise, it never occurred to me that some day I would find it less than perfect planning to face cramming three birthday celebrations into four months. Now, I buy candles in the economy box. My kids learn from each other. At five my son had his first official party—so did the three year old who remembered every detail of her brother's celebration and demanded equal time. Only with the baby could I confine his first celebration to appropriate proportions. (This worked out fine, because for his birthday his sister had given him the chicken pox.)

As a hostess I have learned to avoid other pitfalls of preschool party planning. Picking a time for the party, for example, is no straightforward task. You must decide whether to steer clear of lunchtime (peanut butter for twelve), and you must make it a point to avoid any time that could conceivably be close to nap. It's also a delicate balance between inviting too many children and too few. You want to muster a respectable turnout for your child, but not at the risk of having to employ crowd control measures. Since children never respond to an invitation, this can be tricky. In one case I found myself in the position of rounding up every kid in the neighborhood to compensate for no-shows, and another time everyone on the guest list arrived. I had three adults to oversee twelve children, and it was barely enough. I'm not sure which situation is worse.

But if birthday parties are tough for parents, we are talking monumental angst for kids. For them, birthday parties are more than serious—they are matters of life and death. I can only compare them to the emotional trauma of a wedding which involves so much anticipation that the bride and groom forget to enjoy the actual event.

How else to explain the hysterics brought on by a microscopic tear in the paper birthday crown my three year old got to wear at preschool? Since naps often are out of the question on the day of a party, a child automatically is headed on a downhill slide. It becomes a mother's duty to safely evacuate all the guests before a child blows.

How else to explain the game of musical chairs at my five year old's party? You would have thought these kids were dialing for dollars, the way they scrapped and fought over every chair. In the course of that game, two children were reduced to tears, a third ended up sitting on the ground, and my son staged a walkout and refused to play.

I should have known I was in trouble when a shoving match erupted over who was first in line for the bean bag toss. When the time came to open the presents, the battle lines were drawn. My son put an already ripped open present beside his chair with one hand, and in a feat of manual dexterity simultaneously reached for the next present with the other. The six year old girl who had clawed her way to the head of the bean-bag line reached out and grabbed it first.

"Hey!" shrieked my son. "That's mine!"

"Well," the girl retorted. "You don't get to open every present just because it's your birthday!"

As I said, to the parents at birthday parties fall hard tasks. I had to break it to her that, yes, he did.

13 The Good Old Days I'm Too Young to Remember

THE children, fresh from the playground, sit in a semicircle on their pint-sized chairs and practice yelling "Help!"

"Louder, I can't hear you," says the lady from Junior League, cupping her ear. And so they shout, demonstrating what they would do if a stranger tries to snatch them. Then the children watch grown-ups perform a pretend story about a neighbor man who gives bad touches, and then they watch the women perform it again with a different ending to see what the little girl should have done. They listen to the lady talk about safety. She talks about good and bad secrets, about when to say no, and about private parts. (My daughter lifts her shirt to check them out.) They talk about who is a stranger, how to describe an assailant, and how to recognize an out-of-state license plate.

This isn't police story. This is preschool. My daughter is majoring in scissors and minoring in safety. They used to be the same thing. When my teachers taught safety, they demonstrated how to hold the scissors so the point was covered. Occasionally they would teach about traffic signs. Today when teachers teach safety, they start with scissors and then move on to strangers and drug abuse. My children color in books teaching fire safety, traffic safety, and personal safety. They bring home forms to order ID bracelets in case they get lost or injured. The poster on the classroom door says "*Hugs, not drugs.*"

My son climbs into the car, spies my coffee mug on the dashboard and says: "Hey. You aren't allowed to drink and drive." When Grandma takes my three year old to the potty, my daughter tells her: "Well, Grandma, I guess it's all right if you see my private parts."

Oh, yes, modern children learn their lessons well.

One night a boy selling tickets to a pancake breakfast came to our door during the dinner hour. He quickly replaced food as the center of attention. While my husband negotiated a purchase, the baby became frantic to escape from his high chair and view the excitement. He was smeared with food and I had no desire to free him. So I shouted: "Please come in here, guys. The baby wants to see what's going on."

The boy didn't step inside. He stepped backward, his eyes widened, and he showed every indication of bolting away from our doorway and whatever danger lay within it. So we concluded our business on the doorstep, belatedly realizing we had placed the boy in an awkward position. Now I find myself hoping that my children will be as smart. Our intentions were innocent, but at ten years old that boy was old enough to know that all adults aren't. He had studied the curriculum of survival that teaches not to trust strangers. Now he's majoring in caution.

Our children start out fearless. Sad to say, we have to teach them to be afraid in order to teach them caution. Because babies don't know better, we automatically are afraid for them. We teach them fear of falling, fear of heat, and always to stay out of the street. A five-year-old boy loves dinosaurs, sharks, volcanoes, and monsters. "The bad guys won't get me," he assures you, making a fist. "I'd just beat them up like this and this!" You have to teach him otherwise.

The rules used to be easy: Never leave baby unattended in the car or in the bathtub. But that was before children started disappearing from campsites or vanishing on their way home from school. When my five year old wants to play alone outside and I burden him with instructions before reluctantly letting him out the door, I miss the days when nobody locked a front door.

We live around the corner from the grade school, and daily there is a traffic jam of mothers picking up their children.

"If the kids walk, you never let them walk without friends," one mother instructed me. "Better yet, have them ride bikes.

"Going to school isn't so bad," she added. "Somebody will notice if he doesn't show up. It's coming home that worries me. My son doesn't know it, but I stand on the corner each day and watch to see him coming. Then I go inside and wait ten minutes for him to come in—before I go outside and look again."

The rules have changed. We teach our kids to be wary of strangers and to memorize passwords. "Call me when you get next door," we shout as they run out to play. "Policemen are your friends," I tell my daughter. "No," she shouts. "They are strangers." And so parents are left to draw lines and define distinctions. Some strangers are good, just like some dogs are friendly. It's just that we don't always know which are which. And, sometimes, it's not strangers who turn out to be un-friendly. But I don't want to tell my children it's never safe to trust.

Even an adult can end up feeling wary. I remember once at the library when we were headed toward the car, but my daughter wouldn't budge. Not words, nor threats, nor bribes were going to hoist her fanny from the floor and get her moving to go home. Eventually, I picked her up and carried her screaming and kicking to the doorway. As we made our undignified exit, I caught a strange expression on the faces of several women—a wary watchfulness as they evaluated my actions. And it came to me in a moment of unease: How could I prove this really is my daughter?

Lessons of caution are not confined to the classroom. Milk cartons, with their gallery of faces, daily serve parents a measure of anxiety as we serve children their cereal. Fingerprints are kept by the baby book. Hospitals x-ray Halloween candy. At the grocery store, a woman from a cookie company hands me a coupon and a kit for taking my children's fingerprints. "Best to have them on file," she says cheerily. The coupon comes to me from the cookie company "that cares." Nearby is a computerized store directory. I let my five year old push the buttons while we wait in the checkout line. When the machine isn't telling him where to find the cottage cheese, it shows him pictures of missing children.

I know caution is smart, but I resent how fears can hold us hostage. I know what all this is about. It's not education, it's inoculation. We figure if we tell our children the rules early and often, we can immunize them against an evil world. Then, as they get older, we need administer only occasional booster shots to maintain the protection. I subscribe to the theory, although I'm saddened by the reality. If children are our natural resources, then they are endangered by the moral pollution of our modern world. How about a bumper sticker? Save the children; save their innocence.

Sometimes, however, I am reassured children can do that in spite of us. They seem to learn only what they are old enough to learn. And sometimes they just plain get it wrong.

My son discusses the visit firemen paid to his school. We have a long talk about electrical outlets and escape routes.

"I know what to do if fire catches me," he says.

"OK," I ask, "what do you do?"

"You pray, roll, and run," he answers.

"I never heard that before. Why do you pray?"

A big pause. Then, triumphantly, he tells me: "You pray to God that you're gonna get out of the fire."

I HATE to say that things aren't like I remember from the good old days back when the ice man still delivered, but they aren't. Back in the days when my mail used to come from people I personally knew, certain things looked better. The teen-agers today seem loud and brash. The girls wear tight skirts that embarrass me, and the boys act like the world is their private joke. I don't understand their music, and they drive too fast down the street where my children play. Instead of automatically respecting parents, modern kids seem to decide whether they like you or not. In my neighborhood the children call me by my first name; when I was a child we never knew mothers had them. (I have avoided the issue in front of my children by making reference to So and So's mother.)

In my day we used to think it was a great treat when our parents took us out for breakfast or dinner. More often when they went out, we simply were left behind. My children either complain they don't want to go out for pancakes again, or they tell us where they would like to go based upon the prizes in the kids' meals. At their ages I never knew the names of so many fast-food restaurants, and I guess there weren't that many. McDonald was strictly a farmer.

When I took the children shopping for shoes, recently, the saleslady agreed to wait upon us, but she made it clear we shouldn't expect too much. There was, after all, a sale in progress and we were not the only ones buying shoes. She brought us the sneakers from the back, noting as she handed them to me that she did not have my daughter's size. These were bigger.

"Do the shoes run large?" I asked her. Already sprinting toward another customer, she shrugged in answer to my question.

I can't remember the last time a clerk has offered to fit my child instead of taking my word for the size she wears. It must have been back when "walkers" referred to leather shoes for toddlers and not exercise shoes for grown-ups.

I'm no camel, but the final straw to break my patience has been the report questioning the safety of apples. It reminds me of another report that said some breast milk contains toxins. Motherhood and apple pie may mean America, but apple juice in paper cups means childhood. What mother in America hasn't told her child to eat more fruit? The world is in a fine mess when we are told pesticides may have poisoned apples for our children. I know I sound like Grandma on the *Real McCoys*, but I can't seem to shake this crotchety feeling. I'd like to hear a little more "please" and "thank you" in the world.

When my mother and I went out for lunch recently, I was fully aware of the irony as I unburdened myself to her. She managed to listen to my complaints without reminding me of it.

"You're not getting grumpy," she gently told me. "You're just getting older."

"Oh," I thought to myself. "I should have known something was wrong."

As a mother it has taken me a while to see myself differently from the way I was. But children only see parents the way they are: older than them. You learn to feel like a mother in part because your children can see you in no other way. They can't imagine that you were ever a baby, ever closed your eyes to make a birthday wish, or ever lived before they were there to be taken care of. You yourself have trouble remembering that you ever called for dinner reservations before calling for a baby-sitter. My children find it inconceivable that Mommy and Daddy ever were anything but. Sprung from the womb fully formed and already exasperated, we never were children.

My kids and I spent a recent afternoon playing outside with the newest craze on my block. A hula hoop.

As my son swiveled his five-year-old hips, looking like a pipe cleaner with an itch, I asked him if I could take a turn. "Hula hoops were popular back when I was a kid," I confided. Then I proceeded to strut my stuff. My son blessed me with a look of amazement. "I didn't know they had these then," he responded—emphasis on "then."

A few days later he came home from school describing a "new" game. Earnestly he explained to me how you stand behind the line and try to drop the clothespin inside the bottle.

"I'll bet you never played that," he crowed triumphantly.

"And," I responded silently, "I'll bet you wouldn't know what a clothespin is really for."

SOMETIMES, the more things stay the same, the more things change. I remember when we gave our son his bike. In a timeless birthday ritual, we escorted him out to the driveway where his shiny new set of wheels awaited. Without hesitation and without a backward glance, he climbed aboard and took off to go tooling around the neighborhood. Admiring and envious friends streamed out of their houses. Together they admired the sleek chrome lines and high-tech masculinity of his new wheels. He beamed, and I recognized the latest chapter in that old romance: boy and his bike.

The bike is only 16 inches high and certainly was not his first transportation. At first he scooted about on trikes without pedals, then pumped furiously on a full-fledged tricycle. After that he scorched the pavement on his all-terrain big wheels. But this bike for his fourth birthday was different. He will ride it from his boyhood into his youth. As I watched his straight little back begin to disappear down the block—his legs having sprouted overnight long enough to reach the pedals—I realized nothing of the toddler remains. Although the training wheels on the bike keep him upright, rarely will my son accept that kind of help from a parent.

"Try going a little faster," I advised him in view of his shaky balance.

"Sure, Mom," he replied with a hint of condescension. "You want me to pick up some speed." But first he asked me to knot his jacket around his waist, a serious effort at preschool chic. I watched his wheels carry him away. He wobbled a bit negotiating his first turn, fell a minute later without tears or complaint, and gained speed and confidence as he completed another pass.

Even more than marking his matured physical coordination, the new bike marked his initiation into a different social stratum. The two-wheeler holds him high off the ground and separates him forever from the toddlers who graze at knee level. On it he rides up higher and sets his sights higher. No longer will he ride partway around the block, then rely on Mom to push his bike the rest of the way home. In fact, sometimes he is angry at me and his sister for trailing along after him. And, all too soon, he will outgrow the bike he did not then fully fit. Other birthdays will find him lobbying for a bigger, newer model laden with the latest gadgets. But on that birthday when my son was only four years old, I felt as though we had given him his first set of car keys.

Of course, the girls in my neighborhood ride bikes as well. I see them riding more sedately up the street in pairs, chatting as they go. But it does not seem the same as the hard-driven urgency shared by the boys. A boy's new bike is his ticket to mobility and independence. It makes him one of the guys— even more than the lunchbox he clutches or the backpack he covets. Soon, I thought, my son will ride that bike around the block and across the street, pumping furiously in a hurry to get nowhere in particular but impelled by a physical urge to keep moving. Soon, I was sure, he would be content to walk nowhere, preferring to ride his bike next door for the pleasure of nonchalantly parking it in front of his buddy's house.

Instead, he now scorns his bicycle as much as he used to prize it. His bicycle, that much-coveted birthday present of a year ago, sits dust-covered and abandoned in the garage. It tilts lopsided, balanced by a training wheel.

My son doesn't like to ride it. He says it sways too much and doesn't move fast enough to suit him. He screams in frustration when his wheels spin uselessly atop a bump as he strains to get moving. And he screams at me when I suggest he take a ride on it.

I suspect his anger is mixed with embarrassment. He is the only five year old on the block who has not yet shed his training wheels. The two others, older by six months, roar with reckless abandon up and down the street. Sometimes they flaunt themselves by standing on the pedals as they coast along. The make of the bicycle does not confer status; the fact that it is a two-wheeler does. Sometimes my son runs along beside them. He says he prefers his feet to pedals. He says he doesn't care about riding his bike, and he doesn't want to practice on it. And he stalks off angrily if I bring up the subject. So I have stopped.

I write off his behavior as part of a five year old's personality. The ones I know flog themselves in their quest for perfection and want no part of something they cannot master. The same traits surfaced a few months earlier when my son and I sat together on the floor and practiced tying shoelaces. I took one shoe, he the other.

"You bring the lace around like this," I said as I demonstrated. "Then you wrap the other one over it like this. Then you pull this end out like this—and there you have it."

He tried. He wrapped, he pulled, and the whole thing fell apart. We tried again. "That's right," I said. He pulled—and again it didn't work. His body tensed with anger and he pitched the shoe away.

"Forget it!" he exploded. "I don't want to learn how!" And he hasn't. He can't ride and he can't tie.

I have encountered his stubbornness before. He is not the first child to scream with frustration, overwhelmed by demands that momentarily exceed his skills. First, there was me.

In the 1950s my parents practiced the you-aren't-going-to-stop-until-you-learn method of teaching. When it was time to tie shoelaces, I was hoisted high atop the bathroom counter and instructed. When my fingers fumbled and my tears flowed, I was left there—to learn before I came down. When it was time to learn to ride my bicycle, countless times my father pushed me from behind and then released his hands to allow me to soar. And countless times I crashed.

"You're going to ride to the corner," my father told me as he lined me up at the driveway.

"I can't," I cried.

"You're going to learn," he said, no doubt swayed by his

own frustrations. "I don't want you back inside the house until you can ride to the corner."

"I don't want to ride," I insisted. "I'm never going to ride my bike! I'm going to walk everywhere!"

Eventually, of course, I learned. Now, as an adult, I cannot imagine being unable to balance a bike. But I can remember how I felt as a child, when balancing upright seemed a feat of magic comparable to floating on water—something else I struggled mightily to do. The no-nonsense, sink-or-swim mentality of the Dr. Spock generation must have made an impression for me to remember it so well today. Mostly, I remember how awful it made me feel. And that is why as a parent I do not subscribe to it myself.

I try not to push my son, even when I am disappointed. The day will come when he is ready to do the things he cannot yet master. I compare him to the tulip bulbs I planted in the winter. In his own time, on his own schedule, my son will start to sprout. And when he does, I have no doubts that he will flower beautifully.

14 Battles I Have Lost and Fought

MY one year old sucks his thumb. This may not seem like news to you, but when he started at seven months old it was news to me. I didn't realize, for example, that all of his previous life he had been looking for that thumb. In retrospect I should have guessed. He hadn't bonded well to the plug of latex I previously had been shoving in his mouth. But my other two children came around, and neither is a thumb sucker.

Before I had children, I never had an opinion about the controversies of childhood such as swings, walkers, or pacifiers. Purists advocate doing without. I felt about getting along without them the same way I felt about drugs during childbirth: You do the best you can, and then you use anything you need. I knew I needed a pacifier the minute the nurse popped one into my firstborn's mouth and he stopped crying. Suddenly, I not only had an opinion, I considered the pacifier suitable for bronzing. Instantly, I made a downpayment to buy into the pacifier theory: Give it to a child when he needs it, and then chuck the yucky thing before he's old enough to protest.

With my first child it worked like a charm, but with the second and third, problems began. Eventually I found myself fighting to make my infant son take a pacifier and then fighting to make my three-year-old daughter stop. I could not give it to one, and I could not take it away from the other. Pacifiers and thumbs, I found out, represent an issue of self-control far beyond their function. Too late I realized both can be pawns in a power play.

First of all, I have lost the battle with the baby. Despite my best efforts to the contrary, now that he has found his thumb, he flaunts it. I creep over to his crib and catch him sleeping peacefully with it firmly suctioned in place. I shovel food into his mouth as fast as possible, but frequently his thumb plugs up the opening first. He doesn't cry, this third baby of mine. He just whips that thumb into place and it's as good as shouting: I am tired. I am hungry. I am stressed.

Oh, I have tried to reason with him.

"We don't suck thumbs in this family," I inform him. "Your uncle used to do that and for years your grandpa painted medicine on his finger to make him stop," I threaten him. "Your thumb will make your teeth crooked. Who's going to pay for the braces?" When he puts the thumb in, I wrench it out. But no matter how often I exchange it for the pacifier, the trade doesn't take. Somehow the pacifier keeps falling out. The thumb, which comes attached, never gets lost.

By choosing his thumb over a pacifier, my baby chose self-control. I swear he knew that I wanted him to pick plastic because doing so would put me in charge. He knew that eventually I planned to throw away his pacifier—and throw away his habit as well. When a child sucks his thumb, only he can decide to stop.

The point, I'm forced to admit, is that a baby, my baby, can defy an adult like me. He's bargaining from a position of power and he doesn't even know it. What am I going to do? Spank him? Yell at him? Put him in time out? Unblinkingly he would stare at me with his brown flannel eyes. Sometimes he would give me a toothless smile. The kid could warm up an iceberg. All I can do is melt.

Babies don't seem to understand Mommy is supposed to be in charge. Considering he is my third child, I figured I would make this one conform to my schedule. I would wake him up at my convenience, teach him to be hungry when it suited me, and train him to sleep through any decibel-level of commotion. I've since been evicted from my fool's paradise. Babies always win.

When I pick him up at the baby-sitter, we work our way through an interminable litany of questions. When did he sleep? What time did he eat? How much? Was he happy today? Each day the answers vary, but they translate into the same thing: He does what he wants when he wants. When I first brought my baby to the sitter's she asked me: "What schedule is he on?" I've finally come to realize she posed the question backward. In truth, she needed to know what schedule he has me on.

My daughter, on the other hand, loved her pacifier. The problem is that she would not give it up. Too well I taught her to want the thing; too late I tried to take it away.

No, I did not try to make her go cold turkey. If the truth be told, I did not have the guts. But the serious sucking that once seemed so cute on the face of an infant, seemed grossly out of place on a three year old. Instead of outgrowing her pacifier, my daughter had grown into needing it more. And instead of being able to steal it from an inarticulate toddler, I found myself having to persuade an extremely verbal preschooler to conquer her habit.

At the height of my daughter's passion, we had three pacifiers—one for the car and two for the bed. (There was no sleep for any of us if her pacifier fell under the bed and no backup was available.) Those were supposed to be the only places she was allowed to use them. I kept them up high in the bathroom to be dispensed sparingly. My daughter wanted to make them a steady diet. I knew something was wrong when she began to request naps, and I knew we were in trouble when she began scaling the countertop to get her pacifiers down without asking. I moved them to a cabinet. She taught herself how to use the child-resistant latches. Then she had open access.

Like the season's star debutante, her pacifiers began showing up everywhere—and not only in the best places. She would hold one in her hand while the other was in her mouth. If I demanded one back, she would switch them before surrendering. If they weren't in her mouth, she wanted them within sight. I shuddered to think that just three short years ago I had been the one to encourage her love affair with latex. I had taught her to like the taste, but at the time it had seemed a reasonable alternative to nursing 22 hours a day. Now, at age three, we had to wean her again. So my family began a shaming campaign.

"Big girls don't need those," we said. "Big girls don't use those." We'd applaud whenever she put them away. We laid it on thicker than a Buffalo blizzard. I hadn't felt such urgency since potty training. And she would try. "Tonight," she would proclaim, "I'm going to sleep without my pacifier!" But after the lights were off and the door was closed, she would creep back out and get it. "Can't sleep," she'd explain.

One morning, in a moment of bravado, my daughter renounced her pacifiers for good. With due ceremony she threw them in the diaper pail—and I made a point of emptying it. Beginning that afternoon, of course, she wanted them back.

She cried: "Why is the garbage gone?" She was crafty: "What about the one in the car?" In total desperation, she was tearing apart the house, visiting all the old stashes where they used to be. Close to tears, she banged open cabinets, drawers, and closets in a frantic search. She was an addict craving her fix. She was a dieter trying to find the Sara Lee cheesecake hidden in the kitchen. She was desperately seeking her pacifier.

I understand second thoughts are common. My three-year-old nephew threw his away, I am told, and then went berserk. My brother bought him a new supply, which my nephew hoarded all over the house. Periodically, as he watched Sesame Street in his favorite rocker, he would remove one from his mouth to contemplate it—much the way a man appreciates a fine cigar.

We held firm. Fortunately, my daughter did not realize how easily she could have broken me by sucking her thumb like the baby. And, fortunately, she did not realize the stores sell more. We did not enlighten her. Hers were the only available pacifiers in the world, and they were gone. If she naps a little less willingly now, well, that is a small price to pay.

"The pacifiers are gone," we said. We told everyone within her earshot what a big girl she had become. She felt proud at the same time she suffered from withdrawal. Sometimes now, when she is tired or sad, she mournfully asks again why her pacifiers are gone. But she asks less and less frequently and without true hope. Cheerfully she brags: "I'm all grown up now. I don't use pacifiers."

To my daughter, I believe, her pacifiers were like Valium. They helped her to cope when she felt stressed. They were a nonfattening way of indulging herself when the world got to be too much. They took her back to a simpler time. Her pacifiers renewed her spirits and restored her calm. And, sometimes, I wonder if those plugs are available in a bigger size.

❧

TELEVISION, of course, is another no-win battle. An insidious enemy, it gained entry to my household hiding inside a Trojan Horse otherwise known as Sesame Street.

I will always remember Sesame Street as the best thing to happen to parents since the nap. As a mother, some of my worst days were when a confirmation hearing or inaugural speech preempted the show and destroyed my morning. The segments on each program last only minutes, but the show lasts an hour and manages to hold a child's attention for most of it. When several programs are broadcast back to back, they create a block of time up to two hours during which it is safe to take a shower. Without Sesame Street, millions of mothers across America would never get to the breakfast dishes or read the morning paper. When it comes to making mothers better off, the show has delivered more than any political candidate has ever promised.

If your children hang out on Sesame Street on a regular basis, of course, chances are so do you. My children and I have had long conversations about a monster whose imbalanced diet consists of cookies and a grouch who is not making a statement about poverty by living in a garbage can. I admit to having memorized the lyrics to more than a few songs about rubber duckies, singing in the shower, and boogie woogie sheep. I also know more than I ever wanted to about how crayons and trumpets are made.

Many times, as the characters on Sesame Street cope with frustration, competition, or anger, I've felt their lives have paralleled my children's. With more than passing interest, I followed the adoption of baby Miles by Gordon and Susan. At the time Big Bird experienced pangs of jealousy and the ornithological version of sibling rivalry, I was eight months pregnant with my second child. We quoted Big Bird to our son when we reassured him: "Love is not like bird seed. You never run out." Sesame Street is likely to remain part of my emotional neighborhood. My youngest soon will be the family's newest fan. But although I will let my child watch, I am wiser about what he will be learning.

I used to think the show was like low-calorie cheesecake, providing all of the pleasure and none of the guilt. The show, after all, is educational. But by teaching my children to watch Sesame Street each morning, I failed to realize I was sowing the seeds of my own destruction. Now I realize that while Sesame Street teaches the alphabet, it also teaches children how to watch television. And now I wonder if maybe you can get too much of a good thing.

There is a siren living in our house, a seducer of children and corrupter of minds; its initials are TV. It puts an end to family conversation, vanquishes every toy in the closet, and exposes my children to commercials for products I refuse to buy. It smashes quality time on the rocky shoals of mindless entertainment. Television, I believe, is the reason my children went to their first movie, "Bambi," and were bored. Television has addicted them to fast-paced action.

I see children today running a race to seem older, sprinting toward fads and fashions at an alarming rate. Television and preschools strike me as the likely culprits. Children catch the germs from the tube and spread the infection at school. Sure, children still play with sticks and stones, but the words can start to hurt your sensibilities. Kids can sound like a television tuner gone berserk.

My son will hoist a stick and shout either "Thundercats!" or "Rambo!" He has no clear idea what either means, but like the latest disease, he knows the words are going around. "G.I. Joe, an American hero!" he shouts, to my knowledge never having watched the cartoon show. The neighbor's little girl likewise has a mouth beyond her years. She looks angelic wearing a flouncy pinafore dress with white tights and black patent leather Mary Jane shoes as she rides her bicycle of strawberry-ice cream pink. Smiling sweetly, she boards her bicycle and turns to my son.

"Eat my dust," she snarls, taking off in a squeal of rubber.

My son sleeps wearing the Sword of Power on his new pajamas. His only other choices were G.I. Joe or Transformers. He used to like pictures of friendly animals; now he wants to sleep in a battlefield. I blame the cartoon shows that seem more like commercials in children's clothing. What long arms they have. The lunchbox collection at preschool looks like a rally for intergalactic exploration. My son's box features Battle Beasts, creatures I had never heard of but with whom he is on a first-name basis. My daughter's box has "Ponies" and she already wants to know when she can have her first "Barbie."

Instead of nursery rhymes, my children are just as likely to sing the commercial jingle for a cruise line, a fruit punch drink, or about the joys of clothing made in the USA. (At least that left us open for a discussion of geography and patriotism.) "We will, we will rock you!" they chant. They are echoing a shoe commercial, and they have no inkling why at first their words shake me up. In chorus they sing to me about bleach; they can name every cereal on the grocery shelf. Commercial suggestion has precipitated many a fight in my family. Children believe you should buy a product if you can recognize it in the store.

I blame television, in short, for filling my children's heads with all sorts of garbage I would prefer to throw out. True, I can hardly expect to rear Tom Sawyer in this day and age. Television is a reality of life. But Mark Twain's book became a classic precisely because Tom is a universal boy—even if he never did master the universe.

I have been undone not only over what my children watch on television, but by how much of it they want to see and how hard it is to get them to stop. I wish they would pay as much attention to me as they do to cartoon shows.

We are ready to eat dinner, but my son doesn't know it. Repeatedly I have called him from the foot of the stairs, sent several emissaries to request his presence, and—finally—I stomp upstairs myself to demand it. My son's eyes stare fixedly ahead. Under no other circumstances have I ever seen him sit so still. He responds neither to my voice nor to any other discernible outside stimuli. Finally, in desperation, I resort to the ultimate: I stand in his line of vision. Bingo! He sees me. I know this because he emits an animalistic snarl of anguish.

"Mom," he shouts. "I want to watch!"

Somehow I suspected this, of course, leading me briefly to wonder whether five year olds enjoy stating the obvious or whether they think their parents are incurably dense. In either case, subtlety does not sway me. I switch off the television. I wish I could say I have beaten the boob tube, but I know better. It will be back on again.

Let me state for the record that I believe noneducational TV has its place: Before any other members of the family have gotten out of bed or during the second straight day of driving rain. My son, whom I introduced to the Disney Channel three years ago in a misguided attempt to induce quiet while his sister napped, thinks otherwise. And so we negotiate, making the Treaty of Versailles look like a piece of cake.

"Time to get dressed." "Can you get me dressed while I watch?"

"Time to go out." "Can I watch when we get back?"

"Time to eat." "Call me when dinner is on the table."

Without realizing it, I have retreated from my original no-budge policy.

"I want cartoons," he demands, upping the ante.

"No," I counter. "Mister Rogers or nothing."

Most of the time I wish it would be nothing. And frequently I dig in my heels and just say no. But my son would rather watch a station's test pattern than nothing at all. His attitude comes, in part, from his father who gets his best night's sleep in front of a TV set.

Finally, one day, I decided to do battle. I sang a siren song of my own.

"Can we watch television?" my son and daughter asked.

"After bath," I responded. Then, to sweeten the pot, ingenuously I dangled a bribe: "Would you like to hear a story during bath?" So while they scrubbed and soaked, I told them a story about Jeffery the clown who wasn't funny. All through the shampooing I laid it on thick about his discouragement in the circus. Just after their final rinse I brought it to a heart-warming conclusion in which he wows the audience. I knew I was on the right track because every time I faltered as I invented my instant plot, my three year old shouted: "Read! Read! I mean tell, Mommy! Tell!"

When bath was over, together in a chorus they demanded another story. "If I tell you another story, there won't be time for television," I judiciously informed them. "If I tell you a story, there won't be any television tonight."

"OK," they said without hesitation. "We'd rather hear a story."

And so my problem is solved, I think. Now both children are more than happy to give up television—all I have to do is keep telling them stories.

WHEN it comes to battlegrounds, however, I have spilled more futile blood trying to turn off the lights at bedtime than I ever have trying to turn off the television during the daytime.

"Every day I come home from work and she's sitting there, feeding him," my husband said, as a first-time father. "Feeding him seems to take two hours. She feeds him. He poops. She changes him. He eats again. Then, she puts him down to sleep. Only when he goes down, so does she because she was up all night. Suddenly, I'm the only one left awake in the whole house. Welcome home."

It is always amazing to see consenting adults ambushed and humbled by a helpless infant. A baby, after all, can have only one thing his parents don't: sleep, whenever he wants it. That can be the one thing parents want most. For a mother, getting enough sleep and getting the children to sleep can be her biggest battle.

Sleep is the mental Grand Canyon dividing parents from nonparents; the have-nots from the haves. The latter get to enjoy sleep; the former are obsessed by it. New parents spend a certain amount of time thinking about sleep. Roughly every waking moment. This is not only because they have more waking moments, but because they have so much more to consider: their baby's sleep, their lack of it; their desire to nap, their toddler's determination not to. The quest for sleep becomes a holy grail.

The mother of a newborn has lots in common with a prisoner of war. Waking her up just about the time she cycles into deep sleep has to be an effective torture technique. One night I remember actually telling myself to hurry up and finish my dream before the 2 A.M. feeding. Like millions of mothers, during each nighttime feeding you will find yourself totaling up how much sleep you have managed to snatch. (This may be the time for a refresher course on fractions.) Whoever coined the phrase "sleeping like a baby" had something else entirely in mind. Ask any new parent keeping nighttime vigil beside a bassinet. That baby may be asleep, but he also wheezes, squirms, burps, and cries. Of course, if he doesn't, then the worrying really starts. Usually, once you have satisfied a baby's bodily requirements, he will indeed fall into a deep, angelic sleep. The sleep will be deeper, however, if it occurs during the daytime and while you are holding him.

As babies grow bigger, it does get easier. If it doesn't, pretend it does. Even friends look askance after three months when you still haven't managed to get dressed by dinnertime. Resign yourself to hearing them say how tired you look and forget forever about the past when you used to log a solid nine hours a night.

Eventually, goaded by desperation, you will decide to take charge. First, of course, make it a crusade to teach the baby nighttime isn't daytime. You suddenly realize the fetus that started kicking regularly at 2 A.M. merely was indicating a preference for partying. Remember, eventually every baby succumbs and sleeps through the night. At least until 4:30 A.M. or until teething starts—whichever comes first.

Once you've battled it out over nighttime, then it's time to tackle daytime. Simply sit the cherub down and explain that three 20-minute naps a day won't cut it—especially when it takes 20 minutes to get the guy to sleep. When a child won't sleep, car seats have been known to assume magical properties. A parent's greatest triumph can be disengaging a child from his car seat, taking off his shoes, and carrying him inside to his bed without waking him up. Of course, as with medications, children can build up a resistance. They either learn to stay awake until your mileage exceeds the length of their nap, or they wait until just after you have deposited them on the bed to open their eyes and sit up—alert and refreshed. (Your condition at this point, however, is another matter.)

For the first four years of life, bedrooms can become battle zones. Some children succumb to sleep only when it's practically time to wake up for dinner. The daily naptime skirmish can last longer than the nap itself. Sometimes, it's tempting to abandon principle, skip the nap, and substitute truce for victory. This may mean losing the war. You need his nap as much as he does. His "down time" is your big chance to accomplish everything else you used to do all day. Or, sometimes, a nap is essential to preserving a child's sanity. A tired child is a cranky child. Mine is beyond redemption when he fights with the Velcro on his shoes, and loses. Parents endure a special purgatory during the months when a child who still needs his nap begins to outgrow it. If necessary, throw your child in his room for mandatory "quiet time" and take a nap yourself.

But even once you have given up fighting over naps, you will find yourself fighting over bedtime with a child convinced that whatever you do after he goes to bed is more interesting than what he does in bed.

One strategy is to start hiring baby-sitters so you can go out and avoid the fight entirely. Posted on my refrigerator is a grease-stained list I value more highly than the secret recipe for my special coffee cake. I am, in fact, more willing to share the recipe than the names and numbers on my list. Although I am unlikely to encounter my neighbors at a bake-off, when it comes to baby-sitters we all are potential competitors.

Before you have children, it takes no genius to deduce that

as a parent you will require the services of a baby-sitter. What you cannot anticipate is how hard it will be to find one or how anxious to avoid bedtime you might become. In my day, when we were saving up to buy stereos, almost everyone was interested in working for some extra money. Today's compact disc players are not. In my day some of the best baby-sitters were the experienced older siblings from large families. Today fewer siblings experience large families.

There are good baby-sitters and bad. The bad kind finishes the last piece of coffeecake and watches your television more closely than your children. The good kind is intelligent, fun, energetic, preferably older than ten—and generally unavailable. That's because she (or he) is also the ideal date. There is, thus, a small window of time during which most juveniles are ripe for baby-sitting. The cuter they are, the faster they are out of service.

The more hours daily you are home with your children and the more combative bedtime has become, the more desperately you will want to find a good baby-sitter. If you find a baby-sitter who is reasonably good, competency alone will render her priceless. Not only that, but she will be expensive. Rates have tripled since my baby-sitting days. I used to think I really cleaned up on New Year's Eve by charging a dollar an hour. Now I never ask what a sitter charges; I just pay her until she smiles. I rationalize to myself that the therapeutic value of going out to eat slow food with my husband is worth every penny.

So is the value of missing bedtime. Bedtime used to be life's sweetest blessing, a time to cuddle drowsy babies and kiss sweet-smelling bodies. But lately, it's been more like nighttime's curse: an epic battle waged in pint-sized proportions. The change came soon after the children learned to walk and talk—specifically, to run away and to say no. They want to stay up; we want them to go down. Darkness used to be the great persuader, but during the endless months of Daylight Savings Time, millions of children can argue that they can't go to sleep because it's still light outside.

The deck is stacked against parents. Once we get the kids inside, children know to expect such fun-filled activities as bath and brushing teeth. Baths are lots of fun for kids—in the middle, that is. The start and the stop are rocky. Half the time the trouble is getting them into the tub: wrestling their clothes off and waiting for them to finish running naked relay races. The other half of the time, the trouble is getting them out. The only certainty is that whichever kid fought the hardest against getting in will scream the loudest against getting out.

Then comes brushing teeth. If children are willing to do this at all, it's because they see it as an opportunity to either eat the toothpaste or to spit (after rinsing) without getting in trouble. Even after my gripping description of cavities as oral termites, my children remain skeptical that brushing really is necessary.

And then comes the true struggle to actually get the kids into pajamas and beds. My children have, at various times, been either kids of 1,000 excuses (You promised to tell me about God first), or just plain mules (No way, Jose . . .).

I once read an article suggesting why parents might have trouble putting their children to bed. Subconsciously, it said, parents might feel guilty at not having spent enough time with them during the day. Children exploit this ambivalence. Well, in my household there is no ambivalence. We want those kids in bed—usually because they are keeping us up.

We have tried almost everything. We have established soothing routines of books, kisses, and good-nights. We went through a rocking chair phase and a back-patting phase. We've dangled a gardenful of carrots as in: "I'll read that after you have your pajamas on." And for a while we wielded sticks. I have pounded on the wall downstairs to make sound effects as my husband announces Big Chief Potchintoochas is on his way. My own technique includes an ominous countdown from one to three. (I have no idea what I'll do when I get to three, but so far it has always produced action.)

Once the kids are in bed, of course, all is forgiven. They fall asleep almost before we close the bedroom door, thereby transforming themselves into angels. As battles go, the outcome never is in doubt. But the war must be waged every night, and it begins to feel like a hollow victory. So lately, yes, I know what bedtime is. It's the only time I volunteer to stay downstairs to wash the dishes.

15 He Ain't Heavy; I'm His Mother

LATELY, we have been a collection of calamities. My three year old tripped and cracked her cheek on a cement floor. Her black eye is not yet faded. My five year old's forehead was on a collision course with a frisbee, and the cut between his eyes has not yet healed. The way things are going, my children's twice-a-year portrait is about to become an annual event.

I'm also not suitable for framing with my hair at the awkward stage where the layers are not yet grown out. But that does not matter. My husband and I are never in the formal portraits with our children. We have been making a record of their growth; not of our aging.

"You should be in the pictures with your kids," someone once told me. "When they look back, they will want to see you in them to see how you've changed over the years."

Maybe so, but my husband and I are taking these pictures for our benefit—not for theirs. Since so much of our lives revolves around what's good for the children, I am a bit surprised to hear myself write those words. But I am selfish, I realize, about my memories. Like a kid who gets to pass out the cookies for snack, I want to make sure that I get my share.

My three year old watches me get dressed, her eyes sizing me up and down.

"What do you want to be when you grow up, Mommy?" she asks.

"I'm a writer," I answer.

"No," she giggles. "I mean, what will you do after you're a mommy?"

I ponder what to answer as I apply my lipstick.

"Oh, Mommy, you look beautiful," she breathes, with just a hint of adoration.

And then the answer comes to me. After I'm a mommy, I want to remember being a mommy. I will always be a mother, of course, but I will not always be a mommy. A mommy can heal owies with a kiss; a mom calls the doctor. A mommy takes walks with her children; a mom chauffeurs them in the car. A mommy gets kisses for no apparent reason; a mom must ask for them when nobody else is looking. By the time my daughter wears lipstick more often than a look of adoration, she might let me watch her get dressed to go out.

The erosion of my status already has begun. My five year old has started to call me Mom, the same way he has started to squirm his way out of my hugs if I linger for more than a second. Time was when I would take him to preschool and he would hover by my side until I left. He would show me his "work" and promise to paint me a beautiful picture. His sister still does, and she runs after me several times to kiss me good-bye as I leave. My son used to be like that. Now he strides through the door at school and seems to melt away into the activity, totally unaware of whether I have gone. When I search him out, his kiss is absent-minded, leaving me the impression that he allows me to kiss him because he knows it makes me feel better.

"Don't you want me to kiss you good-bye?" I ask.

"Well, Mom," he mutters, "it's kinda embarrassing."

Even when we say good-night, my son tilts his head for a kiss and then instantly snuggles into his sleep position—with his head turned away toward the wall. He is not rude and he is not less loving. It's just that my son has moved on from the cuddling stage. Oh, sometimes when I read him a book, without thinking he still lays his head on my shoulder. And sometimes, without prompting, he volunteers that he loves me a lot. But I used to be his favorite playmate.

Other mothers tell me the process only accelerates.

"We are walking along," says one mother. "I look back and my daughter is walking a few steps behind me. 'Come on and catch up,' I say. But she doesn't. They go through a stage where they don't want to be seen in public with you."

"That's right," chimes in the mother of a fourth-grader. "They're afraid you'll embarrass them. And if you have to go somewhere together with their friends, they coach you on what to wear and what it's all right to say."

"You're not supposed to touch them in public," says a third mother. "Especially the boys. They have to be cool, and parents definitely are not."

It will not be long, I realize, before my son will be telling me what to say and keeping his distance from me in public. Mothers, he will seem to be saying with a deprecating shrug; everyone has to have them.

So I have to collect my memories while I can.

When I leave my one year old, he always does his darnedest to stall the inevitable. As I sit there talking with his sitter, he buries his head in my neck and wraps my shoulders in a hug. Cautiously, after a few minutes, he flips and plops his fanny into my lap. He grins triumphantly and it is clear that he believes I cannot leave if he does not get up. When I pick him up at the end of the day, he comes running. As I hoist him into the air, his face split wide by a grin, he thumps me on the chest as if to verify I am the real thing. His laughter is a joyous sound.

"Sometimes I think you bring him here just to enjoy all that attention," my sitter teases me.

She is right in one respect. I enjoy all that attention. I want to bottle it and save it so that long after the Mommy Years have ended, I can sniff the fragrance of times gone by. In the days to come, when my youngest child will barely break stride when I walk into the room, I want to remember that once upon a time he would come running.

Sometimes my daughter prefers just sitting.

"Sit next to me, Mommy," she commands, patting a spot next to her on the front steps. She rests her head against my shoulder and sighs. "I just want to be with you," she says— and that's fine by me. When I kiss her good night, no matter how long and how often, she always calls me back. "Hug, hug!" she shouts, as if somehow I forgot. But I don't intend to forget. I'm collecting memories to fill the pages of my mind the same way I fill the pages of the photo album or the pages of this book.

Usually every holiday my children will ask me: What do you want for your birthday or Valentine's Day or Mother's Day? And I always tell them that they don't have to give me anything at all. I'm already taking what I want: all the memories I can muster.